THE FORGOTTEN SHORE

A Book of Poetry

by

J. P. Linstroth

Poetic Matrix Press

Cover art and interior art by J. P. Linstroth

Poetic Matrix Press
www.poeticmatrix.com

ACKNOWLEDGMENTS

I am grateful to cousin and poet Ann Townsend for her careful reading of my poems and to my good friend, Paul Gibbard, for his reading of this volume and both for their considerable commentary.

In addition, I must thank and acknowledge the publisher Taylor & Francis of the academic journal, *History and Anthropology*. While I did not directly quote from my article, "Mayan Cognition, Memory, and Trauma" (*History and Anthropology*, Vol. 20, No. 2, pp. 139-182), I did borrow from some of the ideas and stories I wrote about in that article. Moreover, I acknowledge University of California Press for quoting a line from Paul Farmer's (2005) book, *Pathologies of Power: Health, Human Rights and the New War on the Poor* and his anecdote about the Mayan genocide, especially the phrase: "They buried us with our eyes wide open" (p. 4, 2005).

Acknowledgments are given to family members: John P. Linstroth, Sr., Carol Dorgan, Molly Del Re Linstroth and Michael Linstroth and my in-laws, Joe Del Re and Robyn Poarch Linstroth and also to my nieces, Ali and Peyton and Ruby, and my nephew, Bo. Without their love, none of my artwork is possible. My family and their love have supported me throughout all of my life's endeavors and they are everything to me.

Furthermore, much of the inspiration for the poems in this volume are dedicated to the love of my life, Cássia. Additionally, I have written memorial poems to deceased grandparents and they must be acknowledged as well for their unique inspirations in my life, namely, John Henry Linstroth, Margaret Williams Linstroth, Ruth Reno Dorgan, and Ed Dorgan (although a dedicatory poem of him does not appear in this volume).

Thanks for the pre-publication support provided by twenty very special people. Firstly, my family members, John P. Linstroth, Sr., Molly Del Re Linstroth, and Michael Linstroth; so too, friends, colleagues, and former students who contributed to prepublication production; those friends from the College of Holy Cross: Bob Nix, Dave Butler, John Stankard, and Joe Rondinelli; those friends from the University of Oxford: Conor Nixon, Lorcan Kennan, Frank Humphreys, and David Sutton; and my former PhD students: Patrick Hiller, Yanira Aleman, Michael A. Fonkem, and Vitus Ozoke, as well as other friends: Marie Olson Lounsbery, Jurate Murphy, Jennifer McGrath, and Joe Wyman and my editor, John Peterson. I am grateful to each and every one of you for your wishes to see this book to fruition.

There are a couple of other people I need to thank as well, namely, recent acquaintances and friends: Tony Spaniol, Marshall Teitelbaum, Rusiane Almeida, Valerie Lund, Dan DiCurcio, Otto Von Feigenblatt, Jesus Armas, and Lisa Jones.

There are also former mentors at Oxford (who probably do not expect to be thanked): Sandy Ott, Marcus Banks, and Jeremy MacClancy. Thank you all!

This volume of poetry would not have been possible without the dedication and hard work of my editor and poet, John Peterson, Publisher of *Poetry Matrix Press*. I am truly grateful to John for believing in me and my style of poetry. He saw something in these poems presented here, and perhaps me, as well, as the author. John has given me the gift of his years of experience as a poet and editor, and for these invaluable contributions I will be forever indebted.

There are countless other family and friends to thank as well and too numerous to mention here. Please forgive me for not listing you by name here but you know who you are and how you influenced me over the years.

Ω

CONTENTS

THE FORGOTTEN SHORE

AUTHOR BIOGRAPHY

Ω

PREFACE

This book of poetry, *The Forgotten Shore*, represents a labour of love. It was pieced together here and there from years of writing poetry. Some of the poems herein are old, while others are much newer. None of them have been previously published.

In my mind, and on the page, I have tried to create a "mental landscape" for the reader which is representative of my life, my past loves and present amorous interests, my interests in nature, my fascination with art (both as an artist and as an observer), and my fascination with indigenous peoples, as well as my research in the Spanish Basque Country and the Brazilian Amazon. To borrow from Michel Foucault, herein is a created world, an "archaeology of knowledge," if you will. While unlike Foucault, I am not trying to analyze or interpret institutions or power, rather, this book is more of an "archaeology of emotions," whereby the reader is asked to excavate through landscapes of emotions and observations forming what is in many ways both a complete and yet incomplete encapsulation of my experiences.

In my poetry writing, I borrow heavily from Greek mythology as metaphorical reference and as a means of capturing my most personal emotions. For I have gone through divorce, loved and lost, and even so, loved once again. Such is life. To me referencing ancient Greek thought through their mythology somehow brings the reader back to the classics and the very foundations of Western thought. Of course, I am not alone in this endeavor. This is well trodden territory in the history of poetry.

The book is titled, *The Forgotten Shore*, for good reason. It is representative of a sort of mythical place, a place where love is lost, on the one hand, and may not be re-encountered. Maybe it is a desolate island—a shoreline, a beach, somewhere to be left after a relationship, discarded like drift wood.

And yet, on the other hand, there is inherent in this conceptualization a sense of hope. This latter perspective may not be altogether obvious to the reader. While love is lost, and one may find oneself lonely on a so-called "forgotten shore," and perhaps abandoned, there is, nevertheless, hope of leaving such a place and finding love elsewhere. At least, this is the implication in my mind. Sometimes love leaves us on "forgotten shores." The immediate afterthoughts are we may never find such love again. No future love could possibly match what we have lost and so on. But this is untrue. Love may be found again. We somehow find so-called other soulmates and intimate connections. Yet, these are the immediate emotions which come to mind. All of us at one point or other in our lives have had feelings of loneliness and abandonment, feelings of loss and so forth—and as such these emotions form a major part of this book of poetry.

Of course, readers may interpret my poetic lines and find other meanings and these understandings are equally welcome. Sometimes authors are not always aware of what they are representing, even to themselves. In my view, such writings are part of creative processes involving subconscious levels of thought. For some, such thoughts are often difficult to articulate. But this is where the artist enters. Artists, on many levels, interpret the human experience for us and represent these through themselves—whether these are autobiographical or otherwise.

My editor, John Peterson, mentioned to me in our correspondence that my poetry actually challenges the reader intellectually, and as I stated previously, it is meant to be an "archaeology of knowledge" or "an archaeology of emotions." There is a need to dig and dig deeper and dive into the depths of emotions presented on the page. Maybe the language and style used are archaic, or the vocabulary difficult to understand, or the meanings encountered nebulous and obscure. Still, this allows for a broader interpretation, leaving meanings and interpretations in the abstract, whereby the observer, reader, finds their own meanings concealed and contained within the epistemological and ontological direction of the author—myself. From my point of view, such an archaeology of emotions has a universal quality. All (or, rather, most) of us have known some kind of love, which may either be unrequited or real and lost through break ups and so on. But the human spirit is resilient. We look for love once again.

Other aspects of my poetry resonate other experiences. Often, I reference art and the artistic viewpoint, such as my interpretations and perspectives of the likes of Pablo Picasso, Salvador Dalí, Vincent Van Gogh, Paul Gaugin, and Auguste Rodin, for example. As a bona fide lover of all the arts and because I too draw and paint, I feel a need to poetically observe and reference such artists—as I see myself and my work in them and them in me. It is meant to be an artistic dialogue in this regard too.

So also, are my observations of nature whether in the power of rivers as metaphor, or more simply in the smallest of beings such as ants or in our closest pet counterparts as dogs and my love of such canine beings. In my poetry, I have attempted to produce something original and yet appealing to almost everyone, thereby finding a universal voice through the written word.

A few of the poems in this book are memorial poems to grandparents who have passed away and at the same time are ever present. Through poetry I have presented "odes" to them and brief biographies, trying to encompass who they were as people and influences in my life.

Moreover, for me, there was a need to capture my anthropological fieldwork experiences in other poems—such as the one representing the Mayas, or the one representing the Spanish Basques, or those referencing Brazilian Amazonian Amerindians in general.

In sum, *The Forgotten Shore*, is from a certain perspective, a realization of my dreams as a poet and as an artist—an initial attempt and statement—both formed and forthcoming. If in reading this volume you find one poem you like, or find of interest, then I have done my part and accomplished something. You have taken away something, or perhaps understood what I was trying to say here. For all art, after all, is subjective.

Therefore, *The Forgotten Shore*, is a kind of mental journey, meant to take the reader to other worlds, other times, other places, other feelings, and to resonate in the here and now—a personal testimonial, which may at the same time may be universal.

Most of all, and most importantly, this work is meant to be read again and again and enjoyed and shared. Perhaps, it will aid those processing their own personal emotional landscapes and help them to recognize the universality of the human experience in its interesting and varied forms—the how we are in the world.

J. P. Linstroth
Palm Beach Gardens, Florida
October, 2017

Ω

DEDICATION

This book of poetry is dedicated to the memory of Osmar Cordeiro de Araújo and to Osmar's widow, Marly Nunes de Araújo. Most importantly, this book is dedicated to my only and unique muse, Rita de Cássia Araújo de Cordeiro, brigade meu amor da minha vida, Cássia—beijos meu amor para sempre

Ω

THE FORGOTTEN SHORE

THE VEIL

And there the river ran slowly on, green to the other world as the sun had escaped among the palms and the bull ran on surrounding the moonlight in its shadows, the nostril breath, heavy, hot—filtering veils through palms, interlaced moonlight shadows, dark eyes among the white orange blossoms—globes of orange, Paris' golden temptations.

And again the African sun absorbed everything as if swept across the sky in brilliant fury, swallowing Apollo's chariot and the tower of Moorish gold gleamed upon the lazy green waters. Only the "Torre de Oro" and Moorish palms could be seen as vessels passed on and on in memories upon the Guadalquivir, lazy, languid shadows of the brilliant sun, green stretching forward, outward to other worlds—from the Indies they came forth, conquerors worn of journeys past, glories had, legends done, forebodings—and gold upon gold—as the brilliant tower rose upon the green banks, shadowing blue oasis, slow river on and on to other worlds flow.

And the gypsy eyes studied me in shadows, black, hidden among the windings of the narrow streets and alleyways, whitewashed dreams surrounding me and the smell of the orange-blossomed gardens, perfumed the moonlight air as ghosts of kings and sultans intermingled swaying among the Moorish palms.

And the Giralda chanted the cries of Islam's sons, the Giralda wanting to lose its Christian shackles, why must you hide your sweet face with ringing bells, who are you surrounded by these Catholic kings—Oh, Giralda, chant for me, forget thy bells, rise into the desert sun, rise and let me see your black eyes, rise and chant mysterious—Oh, Alah, Alaaah…Alah, Alaaah….
—And the smell of incense burns clouding thy eyes, hooded mask procession passes again and again, coned fraternities, Medieval, and in unity marches, candles burning, trumpets blowing, drums beating in idolatrous chants through the narrowed-streets, under thy eyes—Giralda—Oh, Christ why have you left me?—Pray for me Mary for your son will die, is dying, has died!

And these blossoms filled my sensual being, these white-dove fluttered wings of aromatic wonder and Persian elegance—dreams among the trickling sounds of fountains—forgotten blue shadows—tiled, white-washed—forgotten blue shadows as light plays tricks among the gardens like leopard spots moving constantly in the darkness, searching, searching, for the gypsy cries—to kill the moonlight and the howling gypsy chants—to disturb the blue shadows of the night—and where is the lost gypsy's guitar—I want to hear it.

And where had you gone among these orange trees—and where had you gone in the Persian blue of the night—had the leopard found you playing with its spots—those blue shadows, those orange blossoms, those silver leaves, that ivory iridescent light—Had it caught you running breathless—Had it forced you of its grip—Had it freed you in the night?

Had the blind man's eye showed itself among these illumined scented trees--How will I find thee among these ancient gardens, these Moorish shadows, these swaying palms—Why must you hide your face—Why have you led me violently, blindly into the night following this bull—How come I must go into this ring and where have you hidden among these blossoms?

And you must never climb these walls—these walls, these of the Alcazar—And you must never visit me in my fortress—for you will never escape these scented gardens—Chant for me, help me find my way under the gaze of this blind man's eye—Chant.

Where have you gone? Why have you left me to die in this ring following theblackness?

And where have you left me in your perfumed labyrinth among these aromatic gardens?

Ω

ODE TO A CHILD

To lay on the floor of that room
And look upward at that collage, those shapes, those stars, those crescent moons,
Their twirling forms in tiny circles encompassed within elliptical space...
You my lost face but not forgotten...

The quietude of light in blue strands streaming downward, casting shadows,
Bunny with an ear bent at an angle, the stubby carrot, the stubby cottontail, and
Teddy across the way on the dresser, the little belly outward, the arms askew, the
sown on smile,
Little dresses in the closet, there I lay...
You my lost face but not forgotten...

My little hands, my little feet, my little eyes, my little smile...
May you know the words I never spoke,
May you know the thoughts I never had,
May you know the sunshine I never felt,
May you be the star I never saw...
You my lost face but not forgotten...

Child of mine, I know all the rhymes of Dr. Seuss,
Child of mine, I know the words to so many poems,
Child of mine, I know the tunes to so many songs,
Child of mine, I know the stories of so many great writers,
Child of mine, I know the acts to so many wonderful plays,

Child of mine, I read these words to you, words, just words, nothing more that I
dare now speak,
They cannot capture you, the all of you, who never knew...
You my lost face but not forgotten...

The walls they enclose me now, Teddy and Bunny are here next to me,
And here I lay, here I lay, here I lay...
Through the bars the little pillow, through the bars the tiny blanket, the unopened
diaper boxes,
The bibs in drawers, the tiny milk bottles, empty...
Here I lay...
You my lost face but not forgotten...

Hold my hand little child, let us walk in the green fields together...
Hold my hand little child, my large palm embracing your diminutive digits...

Give me a big hug little child of mine...
Give me a big kiss little child of mine...
Give me a big smile little child of mine...
Let us go together in the green fields,
Let us feel the warmth of sunshine upon us,
Let us watch the birds fly away,
You and I...
You my lost face but not forgotten...

My little cherub, ruddy cheeks, chubby arms and legs, do not run away...
Dream with me in the world of cherubim...
Dream to a time when sister and I blew the dandelions on that green hill...
Dream to a time when I watched brother's tiny red shoes, running round the house...
Dream with me in the world of cherubim...
You my lost face but not forgotten...

Be my face, be my hands, be my mouth, be my breath...
Be these words...
Bathe me in your golden light,
Open up the heaven's gates...
Be these words...
You my lost face but not forgotten...

Here I lay beneath the heavens in twilight's glow, bathed in the blue sleeping land,
Here I lay beneath the stars, how I see you in their twinkling delight...
You my little one, my sunshine, you the golden strands that lift this
darkness all about...
Here I lay beneath the collage of leaves from yonder oak, the stir of zephyr...
Here I lay and wait for coming spring and see all light once again...
You my lost face but not forgotten...

Begin again, speak to me in a happy and carefree face, which is my face...
Smile to me a smile, which is my smile...
Laugh to me a laugh, which is my laugh...
See my eyes, which are my eyes,
Touch me now with thy little hands,
Open up the abysm of my chaos,

Cry with me child, tears which are my tears...
Bathe me in your light, child of mine, and hold onto heaven thy gaze...

Find me solace in your little hands, find my face, touch my smile,
Find me here as I lay, know me where I am…
I am here for you always, I am here, I am here...

Forget me not child of mine, forever yours to hold, these words I speak for you to
know, these words are all I have,
these words are not lost, nor forgotten, these collage of words reach
heavenward,
They float upward, and upward...

These words are forever yours to hold, play with them child of mine, hold them in
your heavenly gaze, they are yours forever, they are mine forever, they are ours
together, forever there to hold…

Ω

ELYSIUM

O Joy, O Fields of Elysium…

Hands skimming over fields of golden wheat, barley, oats…

These idyllic gentle hills of flaxen-gold, shafts alight, fiery, honeyed…

All dressed in white robes…
And angelic voices sing beyond the azure sky, sheltering above, sheep-herded clouds, now gathered, now scattered, broken robins' eggs…

Aeneous light, xanthic pastures, luteous meadows, brilliant ivoried rays, radiate all, albugineous luminosity…

And surrounded by them…
Holding hands exultant…

Raising goblets of finest wines, vintaged by the gods…

Write thy name in gold-leaflet, gilded letters of great poets, of great composers, of great musicians, of great writers, of great sculptors, of great playwrights, of great actors, of great singers, of great painters—Artists Behold!

O Joy in Elysium, let scribe attest thy golden names…

Rejoice All, Hark, Behold Thy Artists All, Elysium!…

For here they gather to read their words, to play their music, to compose their symphonies, to sing their songs, to write their plays, to act on invisible stages, to paint their paintings, anon, all at once…

Muses Behold! Thou Calliope, Thou Euterpe, Thou Terpsichore, Thou Erato, Thou Melpomene, Thou Thalia, and Thou Polyhymnia…Zeus and Mnemosyne have borne thee all…Live in memories…

Floating in albicant garments, upward, levitating, freely, *praktiké* thy art, in the firmament, one by one, rising toward honeyed light…
O Elysium Rejoice! Another artist among you…

Behold! Rise O Rise…
Heavenward…
Rise above mankind…
Rise above womankind…

Rise above all the cobalt skies…
Toward cyanic heavens…

Artists Behold! Another One Among Us!...

O Elysium, Rejoice!...

$$\Omega$$

WALLOWED

Wallowed?...
Wallowed in what?...
In sin? In shit?...
Pray tell, a crumb of stale bread, a sip of vinegar wine…
Where's the priest? Where's Godot?...
Rolling around in my own filth…
But it's mine and no one else's…
I heard the pig root in the garden again today…
I heard Mozart while throwing up again today…
A sparrow lay dead in the field covered in Dali's ants…
Does time wallow or melt?...
I watched black swallows rise and dive and rise and dive…
The air smelling heavy with rain…
Why not Hollowed? Borrowed? Swallowed (birds?)? Hallowed?
I saw a jade snake slowly begin eating birds' eggs, mouth extended, gullet distended…
What's left?...
And Buddha said nothingness and I was afraid to believe…
Only in star dust…
And the gloaming beyond my own eyes…

Ω

REACHING THE SUN

Apollo's greed o'er azure empyrean…

A lifetime of achievement…
To failure…

Ascending the cerulean firmament, higher and higher…
The oceanic abyss…

For being…
For nothingness…

Waxed-pinions…
Dismantled…
Oblivion…

Forever striving…
Pointless aims…

Attaining the zenith…
To the void of chaos…

Aspiring to the apex…
Arising…
Plummeting nowhere…

Icarian dreams…

Ω

PICASSO'S FRAGMENTS

Her white scattered face with flayed fingers, ogling oval eyes, heavily lashed, star gazed…
Finger-nailed tears, yellow-golden jeweled tear…
Green disjointed nose, red mis-angled hat with jagged blue carnation…
A face split into two conjoined halves, yellow-green…
White chattering-teeth, flailing albicant fingers, green stubs, yellowed fingernails…
Streaming black-smalt hair…

A face of utter horror…
A face of absolute grief…
A terrorized disconcerting staring gaze…
A visage forever frozen and collapsing in on itself with imploding ivory digits…
Tremulous sickly niveous fingers and hands…

Is this what you look like in the mirror when you think of me?...
Are you indeed Dora Maar?...
No, otherwise I would hardly know you…

For I know these Sartrean fragments…
Your sadness in Kafkaesque relief…
Why do you weep so?...
Is it for me you wail?...
Or, is it for yourself bawling thus?...
Or, is it for us?...

For there is the us, which can never be…
Never more…
For how will I ever encompass all of your sorrow?...

I can never hope to ever envelop your terror and abject hate…
Do you loathe me so?...
Is this why you grieve?...
Am I not what you thought I was?...
Will your depression last forever?...

I may never be able to comfort or soothe thee as thou dost deserve…

For I am only mortal with all the frailty of humankind, and perhaps worse...
Stop torturing yourself my darling…
You will be alright…
I will be alright…
We will both of us journey onward…

Albeit never the same…

Ω

DIALOGUE IN COLOURS

I dream in yellow…

And I in red…

When I dream about painting, I then paint my dream…

While I shut my eyes in order to see…

***

You must use your imagination and paint from your imagination Vincent…

Paul, I am not you, I have to see the thing in front of me first and then I paint as I see it…

***

Why do you use so much paint?

And why you so little?

Your colours are all wrong…

And so are yours…

***

I the monk…

You the scoundrel…

***

Why do you scowl so like Jean Valjean—on the prowl, to pounce perhaps, a thief in the dark?

And why are you so much like a monk—aloof and secluded and shorn as a sheep?

***

The little yellow house, smelling musty, of sweat and mould, turpentine and pigment and the cloudy air of pipe smoke, heavy and pervasive…

But we welcomed each other as brothers and hugged…

Then we got drunk on wine…

***

There is something to the Japanese prints aren't there Paul?

I think so, bright colours, the shapes, the bodies just so, posed just so…

***

When I paint there is a kind of fever that overcomes me and I am obsessed with the composition until it is done…

***

There is something to Cézanne, perhaps he is the Master of us all Vincent, he moves me with his style and forms…

Not to me Paul, timid I would say and economical with his brushstrokes…

***

Not to me…

Art requires a philosophy and philosophy art, otherwise what of beauty?

***

I put my heart and soul into my all of my work, day and night, I toil like the farmer in his fields, many times I cannot sleep and I am always restless and in the process I am losing my mind…

***

Let's drink to art…
"To art!"

***

And he lay there in a pool of blood, the ivory pillow soaked, now turning a brownish rusty ochre colour…
He lay there curled up in a ball, with the covers up over his head…

There was blood all up and down the wooden stairs, it was smattered about like crimson paint blotches everywhere, on the red tiles, smeared on the blue doors…

***

And the policeman asked me what I had done…

"Nothing!" I said in firm astonishment.

He had given his ear to that prostitute, Rachel…HIS EAR!!!???

***

He will always be to me the painter of the sunflowers….

The golden man with the red beard, cropped hair, smoking his bowl of tobacco, glaring at me happily…

Just the other night he threw an emerald glass of absinthe at my head…

***

And now in sultry Tahiti, I sometimes think of Vincent…

The smell of saltiness as palms sway from sensual oceanic breezes and I lay in blue shade and shadow…

But I remember the dry zephyrs of Arles…

`

And here I am with these magnificent creatures, tanned and golden bosoms, dark nippled, honeyed skin, and flowery robes—magentas, navy-blues, royal purples, turquoises, and cerises…

Pink and red hibiscus carefully placed above delicate little brown ears, their black sleek hair…

When they brush it or wash it or fold me over in it like great black feathered fans, I am transfixed, and mesmerized…

In a dream…

And so in my own way I try to capture this ecstasy…

It is being surrounded by a golden harem of goddesses like Odysseus enraptured by Circe and her nymphs...

I do not have one wife now but many lovers, each more beautiful than the last…

Ebonied tresses softened by coconut oils…

***

And he shot himself and I could not save him…

If only he were here that red bearded little Dutch man…

This is my Polynesian Elysium…

It could have been his too…

$$\Omega$$

MAYAN MEMORIES[1]

They buried us with our eyes wide open…

We were Ixil Mayas…
We were Q'anjob'al Mayas…
We were Chuj Mayas…
We were K'ich'e Mayas…
We were Achi Mayas…
We were Mam Mayas…
We were Q'eqchi' Mayas…
We were Kaqchikel Mayas…

We were 200,000…
We disappeared…

They buried us with our eyes wide open…

They were all lying on the ground with their hands tied behind their backs…
Some were dead, some were barely moving and alive…
The soldiers were hitting them with machetes and blood was everywhere…
They gathered all the women and children into one thatched-hut and burnt it to the ground…
The screams were horrific and were deafening…

They buried us with our eyes wide open…

The guerrillas came one night to the house of my uncle asking for food…
We called these people, "the men who came at night"…
They were trying to persuade people to join them…
They carried away three men I knew…
My uncle was one…
When they did not come back, their families and mine went looking…
We found them in the cornfields…
Some had arms chopped off…
Their heads were barely attached to their necks…
Then the soldiers came at 4:00 am…
They started shooting at all of us, terrified screaming everywhere, running women and children…

The next day we buried so many of them in the fields…
We did not perform any ceremonies…
        We were too afraid…

They buried us with our eyes wide open…

        I was in the field on the hillside picking maize, beans, and peppers…
They came from behind me and took me, three of them, soldiers…
        All of them laughing, laughing, laughing at me…
They put a scarf in my mouth to muffle my screams…
        They ripped away my red *huipil* and *corte* and tore off my underwear…
They were heavy on top of me, so heavy, and they had bad breath…
        One had a moustache and sideburns…
All of them kept laughing taking turns, holding my arms, holding my legs…
        I was shaking all over and could not stop trembling…

They buried us with our eyes wide open…

        My cousin disappeared one day…
One day he just did not show up and we never heard from him again…
        By then the army had burnt down our house and we were forced to stay with my grandmother…
        Then one day the army brought my uncle in a coffin to our house…
His head was still bleeding…
        My grandmother picked up his arms and she could still move them…
They were flexible…
        This is when we knew he was killed not so long ago…
That is when we decided to leave to the mountains…
        Then we left for *El Norte* for good…

They buried us with our eyes wide open…
        Our souls will never rest…
They buried us with our eyes wide open…

Ω

MEU CASSIA[2]

Eu Canto O Seu Nome…
I sing your name…Cassia…to the longing wind, to the opulent moon, to the billions of stars in the heavens, to the cascading comets…

O Cassia you are my crimson-purplish sunrise and my carmine sunset…

O Cassia, the sun caressing your golden skin along that forgotten shore…

Eu Canto O Seu Nome…
I sing your name Cassia, Cassia…to the writhing expanse of the muddied Amazon, thy Anaconda, grasping and crushing god, and mother of my people, winding and coursing through your veins…

Eu Canto O Seu Nome…
Lost am I when I sing your name Cassia, Cassia, Cassia…In the evergreen rain-forest lush, the greened leaved walls closing in, the throaty-hooting roars of the howler monkeys belching your name Cassia in the canopy above us, the shrieking Harpy Eagle calling your name above in the wind in mid-soaring flight, the Hoatzin pheasant chants your name Cassia hidden in brush, the Brazilian Tinamou whistling Cassia, jungle unbearable humidity, sweating soaked through, and alive everywhere in sounds seemingly chanting Cassia O Cassia…

Eu Canto O Seu Nome…
The curves of your body, full-breasted, dark-nippled, black hair undulating in half-blue shadows near the grunting jaguar, bending forward, bending backward, the *preta* hair, black as night sky and the jaguar grunts your name Cassia in the blue shadows, its spots now black, now blue, now bodied golden in the sun, undulating sable-splotches in blue-shadows, animal sounds and cries, the black eyes of Amerindians, painted and feathered, the shaman's chant to animal spirits, evoking your name Cassia like a mantra…

Eu Canto O Seu Nome…
To the palm tree-ed beaches of Bahia, where Afro-Brazilians dance and sing with their Candomblé creed, and the lull of the ocean waves whispering Cassia, and the dancers become possessed by the Orishas, uncontrollably shaking and whitened-eyed, and the drums beat out your name Cassia, Cassia, Cassia in deep trances as your black eyes gaze upon browned-bodies sweating and glinting in the heat and embered-sun and chanting and calling out to the Orishas as the drum beats get louder and louder and louder, and your name being called out Cassia, as if to their goddess…

20

Eu Canto O Seu Nome…
I see you in the streets of São Paulo as the multitude of cars honk your name Cassia, Cassia, Cassia…throughout the sweltering streets and gleaming sidewalks, trashstrewn, and skyscrapered shadows, blue on your face, as you move through the thronging crowds, pushing through in your beautiful black dress and your flowing ebony hair slightly-fluttering in an ever so gentle breeze as the sun finds its way around corners of immense buildings, painting you golden, and then more buildings hiding you in their shadows, daintily lifting your Louis Vuitton bag for shopping, a slight twitch of your delicate Roman-Portuguese nose, descendant of the *Sertanistas*, fighting and enslaving Amerindians, conquering the interior—O Brasil, how I weep for you…And the faceless Indians running, running, running…And you running too with them as the shaman's intoxicated ayahuascan chants in his shadowed hut dreaming afar…Cassia, Cassia…

Eu Canto O Seu Nome…
Meu Cassia, Meu Cassia, Meu Cassia…moving in jaguar blue-shadows, your ebony hair flying through green expanse, your blackened-hair wetted from brown-mud-died waters, in a sudden splash arising forth like an Indian-Venus, breasts glistening honeyed in the overpowering sunlight…

And you Cassia, I sing your name but the jaguar is close by, hot breath, panting, blue-shadowed, black splotchy-patches, and your black inky-eyes following me, hiding from me, if I sing your name Cassia, Cassia, Cassia…Will you come to me radiant like the dazzling ever-bright sun, or will you hide in your blue shadows…Memories of touches, memories of longing kisses in azure shadows, O how I want to ravage you with my lust…O Cassia, Cassia…

Eu Canto O Seu Nome…
O Cassia my Cassia burning yearning for thee…

Eu Canto O Seu Nome…
O Cassia my Cassia, my unbearable aching heart lost upon that forgotten shore…Where can I find thee O meu Cassia?

Eu Canto O Seu Nome…
And I can still hear your name Cassia, Cassia, Cassia in hushed silence recalled in the windscaped sketches of my mind…

Eu Canto O Seu Nome…Cassia, Cassia, Cassia…

Ω

A FORGOTTEN BEAUTY

I tried holding onto thee but you were armless like the Venus de Milo...
And cold my sweet as whitest alabaster and the Carrara marbles of Michaelangelo...
So you did become such...

And yet still...
Once you did hold me transfixed...
Your gaze upon me sunlit rays piercing as arrowed projectiles...
Like Saint Sebastian—again and again and again...
Pinioned by your darkly eyes...

A face so fair whereby the cherubim encircled you with their angelic praise...
And that rosy hue of yours...
Your cheeks as such to make Aphrodite weep...

You foamed forth upon me...
Elegantly, rising above all others...

While the sea nymphs sang your praises...
And old Neptune calmed all the seas about you...
All they could do was but stare...

Oh but not I my love...
So much more...

I saw you as I hold this photo now of you...
And the azure skies opened up as glaring Zeus rumbled...
And Thor greatly hammered out all the darkened cumuli above you...
Flashes of you now my love...

It was my eyes who caught yours somehow...
Impossibly how...
You in my forever mind...

You my unrequited amor as Lady Roxane to Cyrano de Bergerac...
A fate not to be...
At least not for me...

You above the others, full lips glistening as dew in morning gold...
You above the others, bosomed womanhood...
Full and fertile to the rage of Ares...

You above the others, how my heart held you dear...
Cherished by your smile—ivoried gleaming...
          The whole world awakened by your gaze...

While you were there in my bed...
          Disrobed beneath our rumpled sheets...
                    Your loving head upon my chest...

And then our nectared wine soured to vinegar...
          Almost without warning...
          The omens were difficult to discern...
          Momentarily...
But the bread too had become stale...

          The priest long gone to bless anything...
          And our union rendered now impossible...
          The Host broken and scattered about the ground...

And so now it is near unbearable to tell...
          How like the ashen Mona Lisa you became..
                    A simple but blank stare impractical now to read...

You so suddenly faded from my world in shadowed dreams...
Glimpses of you in hazy glows...
          Bodies entwined from remembered embrace...
          Faded now into a fog unseen...

Your face now in moonly orb like a Japanese Noh mask...
Where the night has taken me once more...
Away from you, away from you...

          A love now scorned...

          Only now may Hades allow me to forget...

          The sun no more...

Gone, gone, gone...
My alabaster queen you are no more...

And I run into your arms once more in my dreams...
Only finding your limbless self...
Helpless now...

Catch me not, my soul affray...
For beauty hath dashed me upon its shore...
The shore of forgotten love once more...

Ω

AMNESIA

How soon we forget…
Had you drunk from the River Lethe?…

How soon we forget…

By spending wasted time wandering and roaming…
And ponder thusly forever more, wondering 'til the gloaming…
A fruitless endeavor, what for?…

How soon we forget…

All those who come before us…
And nothing from their silent chorus…

How soon we forget…

What love is, what love is not…
In debt to what behoves us and to do what we ought…

How soon we forget…

What our toils mean…
And ne'er an hour to spoil them upon a wanton scene…

How soon we forget…

Life is filled with strife…
Yet with happiness may beget a better life…

How soon we forget…

A slight caress known to be rife with emotion…
And thus shown a radiant light to redress life's blight and commotion…

How soon we forget…

There may not be a morrow…
But neither does life need to be burdened with sorrow…

    How soon we forget…

Many of us do suffer…
Though we may eschew the tougher by aiding the other…

    How soon we forget…

It is in our power to beget the better…
And scour away the bad with no regret of life's fetters…

    How soon we forget…

To hewn the hours with care and not fret or despair…
Too soon to be strewn to winds and sea…
Rather commune with one's fellow and rescind what is beyond thee…

    Lest we forget…

    Beware of the River Lethe…

Ω

THINKER IN HELL

Fisted to chin…
All my muscle, sinew, force, right elbow to left knee, left arm languishing
on the same…
Sitting upon this precipice…
O'er the abyss…
I am inflamed, embered, and burning…
My thoughts of you run wild…
Yet neither here nor there…

Rodin you never knew me…
Dante what do you know of hell?…
Neither am I Lorenzo de Medici in meditative repose…

Lost in tumultuous, painful introspection…
Lost in time, lost to time…

I cannot move from this solid, unyielding escarpment…
All these damned souls…
Forced to wonder…
How could I have?…
She scorned, my wanton ways…
My many vices, my foolishness…

Dumbfounded…
All muscle, sinew to fist…
Forever furrowed brow…

She so lovely, now gone, gone, gone…
Missing her now…
Done her wrong…
This burning bothers me not…
Embered and inflamed…

Wails and cries of other damned souls…
Gnashing of teeth…
Sounds horrific to behold…

And yet beholden to no one…
Only to her…
Angry, enraged, saddened, sorrowed…
Affixed here forever and ever…
Time without end…
Limitless, boundless, infinite reflection…

Shamed…
Obligatory, imposed contemplation…
Forgotten in rumination…

Memories, good and bad…
Natheless, mind wanders to the hateful…
Mine mind wanders, times long past…

O solitude…
God forsaken me…
Mine disbelief…
Retribution…
I know not what…
Tautologies…
Over and over and over mine thoughts…

Neither focused, nor recalled…
Haze of the oblivion…

Obsessed, possessed am I…
With her…
Hitherto, all without her…
Here, here, here…
Now, now, now…

Forged on this rock…
Forever more…
Never shall she meet me on that forgotten shore…
A shore without end…
Endlessly beautiful, snowy-whitened sands…
Azure sea…
Mine mind adrift…
Lost…

Ocean tossed amidst blackened waves…
Whitecapped forebodings…
Drowning, drowning, drowning…
Cyclones of hate…

Will I know her ever more…
Nay say they, nay say they…

O lost, O lost, O lost…
Never to reach that forgotten shore…
Her gone, absent from me…
Imposed lonesome isolation, friendless, abandoned…
Dissipated, disappeared, vanished…

Mine mind's eye…
Into nothingness…
Into nonexistence…

I cannot seek her ever more…
For time has forgotten me…
Lost on that forgotten and nameless shore…
Shackled, encumbered…
This lonely crag…

Here beyond time…
Here beyond memory…
Here, Here, Here…
And no more…
Always to be forgotten on her deserted shore…

Ω

MY LITTLE ANT ASTRAY

My little ant astray…
Where are you going?...
Don't you know the world is filled with foreboding?...
Circle and circle as you may have you lost your way and your nest?...
Is this instinctual rehearsal a little test?...
Are you a scout whereby you must wander about?...
Beware of being prey as you go astray…
Have you scented food and left a trail for others to follow?...
What is meant by your mood and will others collude with you in your chemical braille and return to your little hollow?...
My little ant astray, you may instead meet my shoe and in that way end up dead…
Or, will you again struggle through another day, my little ant astray?...

Ω

SISYPHEAN DREAMS

To dream beyond oneself…

The great incandescent orb of Helios, his risings and fallings…
And argent Selene, the ebbs and flows of her tides in azuline light…

To dream beyond oneself…

Ascend to the great summit above…
And hurl to the great abyss below…

To dream beyond oneself…

Reach the pinnacle…
And be cast downward…

To dream beyond oneself…

Aspire with hope…
And told no…

To dream beyond oneself…

A powerful yearning…
And an absolute spurning…

To dream beyond oneself…

To acquire knowledge…
And realize ignorance…

To dream beyond oneself…

   The, I am, who I am…
   And the, I am, who I am not…

To dream beyond oneself…

Ω

LOXAHATCHEE RIVER

O great Loxahatchee, "River of Turtles," as Seminoles named you so long ago…
Hydra-headed forking inland from your brackish waters emptying into the sea,
splitting northward and westward at your headwaters…

I have seen you in the midday sun glinting silver and coffee, turbulent…
I watched a white-black osprey gliding and hovering, then swooping-down, diving,
for a fish, seizing it with its talons, and off the waters, to beat wings-downward to
hungry-downy chicks in a twiggy-nest, Christ crowned, in the upper-reaches of a
v-crux of branches on a charred-skeleton tree denuded by lightning…

I spied black alligators on white-sanded banks slide into your tea-tinted waters …

I watched box turtles—plop, plop, plop—into your hazel waters off a rotted green
algaed-log, knotted and protruding like a broken arm with a black bone exposed…

I watched black-shadowed alligators' outlines skim the surface, moving ever so
stealthily like submarines, partially elongated heads and tails silhouetting the
surface, tipped-inky fingerprinted ridges of crags, moving ever so slowly through
the murky waters, kings of this river…

And I surveyed cumulonimbus piling higher and higher like grey cotton-clumps
into fierce thunderheads, tops grey and bottoms ebony until dimming all light as
night, pregnant with rains, flashing white-striking blazes luminescent against black
moccasin clouds, writhing in undulations eastward, and the smell of rains heavy in
the air as a flock of gulls winged steadily eastward, fearfully….

Then the pelting rains came, downward and downward, heaving drum beats in
millions of tiny-splashes, shimmering in a grey haze across the river, a downpour in
fog, dancing on black waters until all became like smoky grey steam…

In your calm, I saw white egrets fish in the shallows of your tea-tinged banks,
daintily stepping in the shoals near emerald stalks of sawgrass, with swirling water
hyacinth and water lilies close by, black-stick praying-mantis legs still, then long-
yellowed beaks spiking perch and juvenile bass…

In your Stygian waters I witnessed the slow motion of time, of epochs long past, and
eons and eons ago, of some begotten primordial age, an era of dinosaurs devoid of

humankind, witnessing death and rebirth, again and again, cycling into each other infinitely…

I contemplated how dancing mayflies flitted on the water's surface, near knotted cypress stumps, old man's submerged black-knuckles, as a multitude of catfish roiled and quaffed at the surface…

On a moonlit night I beheld a moon hanging like a golden lantern, fossilized amber, hiding and haloing in pasty-grey clouds, and ever so delicately a dragonfly, silver-winged fluttered down onto the glass steel-black surface as a large mouth bass gulped upward in one motion in a gurgling implosion on the darkling river…

Near the banks I can see the verdurous undergrowth of cabbage palms and blowing pine scrub and more on the distant horizon, the rising majestic slash pines ochered and top-tufted-green-coniferous, pine flatwoods in the beyond reaching to cyanic skies…

Not far away in the sylvan copse of live oak trees with silver branches, trunks partially covered in greenish-whitish lichens, their thin spaded green leaves shading the cabbage palm scrub, I observed a mother deer and her white-spotted fawn in blue shadows waiting out the day's heat…

Near another live oak grove, a couple of tusked wild hogs, burnt sienna and black colored, rooted around the feet of the trees turning up black-sandy clots with hundreds of hooved-prints circling round and round, rooting for acorns…

In a sandy patch of the forest where a slash pine lay rotting, I examined a large diamond-back rattler with acute-obtuse angled, rhombus crisscrossing patterning, chestnut-white lying hidden beneath the coolness of the log waiting for some unsuspecting woodland mouse…

In a clearing amongst a patch of slash pines, throwing long-blue shadows, turkeys gobbled and warbled, males strutting with their fleshy pink-blue turkey necks and heads wagging to and fro, with red-pinkish wattles oscillating, and the unmistakable —worble—rrr-kk, worble—rrr-kk, worble—rrr-kk—scratching and pecking at the ground, proud mahogany feathered birds, fanning-tail feather struts, and in the heat kicking up yellowing-dust from the rotting heaps of burnt-umber pine needles…

And further downstream near where the sand pines burnt down from lightning strikes, charred wintery-leafless skeletons stark against azure empyrean, there rose a host of coconut palms, their green splayed swaying combed fanning fingers and their hoary twisted trunks like dried wet-noodles, haphazard on some broken blue-plate, where wisps of traveling pallid clouds meet the cobalt sky, welcomed my passing as a black cormorant stood with its ebony wings akimbo…

Onward still a pair of charcoal colored coots with red and yellow-tipped beaks squawking—owpf, owpf, owpf—as wide-ashen trunked royal palms looked on in stalwart majesty, their large jade-emerald palm fronds reaching outward like great green eagle wings…

At the river's end and near the Atlantic in its most brackish-salty waters, where mangrove trees grow, caramelled branches like hundreds of ladies' fingers dipping for manicures, or rather more like skinny brown-bowlegged women lifting up their virescent-skirts in the thousands of some verdant metropolis, I studied fat-nosed, menacing, female bull sharks moving upriver to give birth to their pups among the mangroves to provide for their cover and I peered at two manatees, a mother and her calf, floating listlessly like grey balloons in the gloomy waters, grazing where the sea grasses remain, the white-scarred striations on the mother's back from boat-propeller blades…

And on this same great river, the Loxahatchee, there once lived a "Wildman," named Trapper Nelson, who traded in furs in the 1930s, making his living in this riverine environment, and after the Second Great War, made a tourist attraction of his river establishment by renting cabins and rowboats and by handling snakes and wrestling alligators, just like the Seminoles did off Alligator-Alley, but in the end he became paranoid and a swamp hermit, going out like Hemingway, poor "Papa"…

There are always stories here, many stories…
Such as the one about the poor Boy Scout being eaten alive by an alligator and taken down under into the blackness, never to be seen again…

The tales are endless…

The river is a small, wonderful world in and of itself…

I know this river, the Loxahatchee, in all its many guises, and where it hides in its black and blue shadows…

It hides in its coffee-colored tinctured undulations and rippling movements eastward…

On bright sunny days it is silver-black glinting, shimmering…

On full-moon nights the waters are sheen-white and ebony ruffled…

It hides in its tea-colored banks of white-sandy shoals…

It is a river unlike all other rivers…
It is the Everglades in miniature…
It is life primordial…
It is continuous…

It is like the River Styx, as it knows death…
But it also knows life, teaming with life, rife with creatures great and small, with a profuseness of greenery, foliage, and verdure…

It knows the sun, it knows the moon, it knows the tides, it knows the rains, it knows fires, it knows hurricanes and over time many of its inhabitants have come and gone and come and gone almost forever…

It is a river knowing dry seasons and wet seasons…

It is a Floridian river…

It is my river…

It may be your river too if you quietly paddle through it to find its numerous secrets in its many recesses and curves…

And like many rivers it is reminiscent of times long forgotten, a hidden wilderness, special natural beauty, flowing onward and onward to the sea…

Behold, the Great Loxahatchee River, one and all!...

Ω

THE LAND OF LUST

I know a barren land…
the land of lust…

and ashes to ashes and dust to dust, unabatedly and nakedly fondling, forbidden…
where men and women must thrust and thrust degenerately and wickedly and lust
to no end unto oblivion…
laden with disgust, a wandering and misspent wend…

alas, a land where unrepentant Eros broke his bloody wings long ago and his
passion-ed arrows then splintered asunder, a cherub of abomination…
where Aphrodite became repellent and ugly from wrong and woe, and wanton-ed
flings, blundered, ashen winters and Ares a barrow, lost her dominion…

a land where Dorian Gray's painting evermore hideously rotted…
a land where all whoever come are forever and ignominiously besotted…

a land of lust whence all who enter forever mistrust their lovers, evermore jealous of
their lascivious beloved…
and where desirous love is forever repelled thus and lotted…

beware the land of lust and blame, where lovers combust from inflamed desires,
their lives forevermore blotted…
a land of shame, mired, and ever a saltern as the wife of Lot…

I know a barren land, the land of lust…

Ω

ARES, HEPHAESTUS, AND APHRODITE

Am I your Ares or Hephaestus?...
Will you love my golden body, perfect, shapely, hardened, muscled from many
a war...
Is that what you want ever more—your beauty, nary withheld, lustrous...

Will I pierce you with my arrows straight and true?...
Or, will the javelin equally do?...

Or rather, forge you a life?...
Forge you diamonds and rings, necklaces and other pretty things?...
For you know I am lame, mostly of my essence for you, all the same...

Will you love me intensely like no other?...
Will I make you blush with scandalous words?...
Will you love me, burning, desire, embered in your heart?...
Or, will you bid me *adieu* and love another?...

O Olympus gaze upon thee...
Beauteous boundless, as no other...
Fair skin, raven hair—endless, craving, kisses thy *Kypris*...[3]
My supreme gratification, infinite pleasure, goddess of desire...
A bosom beyond compare, with others inviting their ire...
Sometimes skin, honeyed golden, sometimes not, as pale as winter snow...
Timeless beauty, natural, a constant pink-petaled stream, forever flow, and if you
want it so, as you do seem, I will always be your beau...

O Aphrodite, Hephaestus and I are brothers...
Whence mine own arrogant, conceited, pompous...
His humble, vulnerable, masterful craftsman...
Mine own frivolous and vain...
His deferential, respectful, and diffident...
And yet, not without confidence...
I have known other women all the same...

It is only for you have I rapt attention...
O my Brazilian Aphrodite, née Portuguese conquistadores, née Amerindians, née

Afro-slaves, not to mention—other Europes intertwined…
You Aphrodite flowering laurels, anthophilous, Nature's bounty…
You Aphrodite, so nimbly you disrobe—apodysophilia…
So too hydrophilous from seaing foam, effervescent, emergent on azure waves…
Giant cockles, envied all…
Your cynosure assured as no other, without contention…

And so you must choose, my radiant ebonied tresses, gorgeousness, delightful, elegance…
Full breasted, more alluring than Hera, more ravishing than Athena, more charming than Artemis…
Neither Helen of Troy, nor Nymph, nor Muse may compare to thee, thy beaming, twinkling, goddess from the sea—only know me, only me…

Mine philocaly and philogyny, all for thee…
Take you in mine arms…
In your dreams somnambulant…
For Ares and Hephaestus are the same, brothers true…
Yet neither one of us will ever possess you…

You my wild child do not run away…
Assail me with your beguiling sway…

I god of manly passion—fiery, fervid, explosive…
Watch my arrows true…
And my spear making its mark upon you…

Or, shall I catch you in imperceptible golden-sparkling-diamond gossamer with him I loathe…
Helios shone upon them, trapped embrace, unclothed…
For I have forged your name in the stars, O Aphrodite, my goddess, my sublime, my softest pleasure, my greatest joy…
Do not make me just your ploy…
Do not look upon me with sorrow or disgust, since my craft is only thus, perhaps immortal but not next to thine—for only you may strike me low…
No escape from thine night eyes, shifting here and there…
Once upon me and then like flight…
Do not hasten away, I beg you with all my might…
For I am more to you my love than Apollo's radiance to Daphne, caught, honeyed, glowing brilliance, Bay Laurel now and no more…

Is victory mine?...
Are you divine?...

And my passion for thee is ever more...
I have caught you up in my soldiering strides...
I have caught you up as my loving and devoted bride...

Will you rather love the humble me, forging forward in craft and wit?...
Or will you love me gallant, bronzed, striking figure in form, fiery and all about to storm...
To rapture thee beyond the norm—blissful, ecstatic, exultant...
You my wondrous woman, resultant...

How will you know me thus?...
Continuous hammering of your ebullient heart...
My tempest storm, you blossoming warm into cumulonimbus...

Will your passion ever go away?...
Shall I find you for another day, and sway you with my love...

Who am I to you, my perfect tenebrous Aphrodite—Ares or Hephaestus?...
The one almighty, or the one lame, meek, and submissive, spaking thus?

How shall I know you in years to come, my ebonied mane and face so fair, put all to shame?...
Mine libidinous tears summoned...
Will you yearn for me as you do today or will I lose you in ocean yonder, abandoned...
With only hope, may your heart grow fonder?...

Battled or encumbered, which?...
Fierce or modest?...
So both Ares and Hephaestus, am I...
Hearts yours, as both we do implore...

You my verdant spring, you my radiant sun, you my full-moon aglow...
For yes, it is I with whom you know and what you'll do...
Not run away from me and transform into Apollo's laurel tree...

On and on we shall go, celestial, heavenward and divine, mine contradictions all mine…
And only you will ever make my heart to chime, and you alone will make my life rhyme, for together we shall climb that mountain yonder…

On to Olympus my Aphrodite, you my bounteous, stunning, omnipotent, supreme…
And low behold, your husband, manly to the core, and the other unassuming evermore…

For I am Ares and Hephaestus all the same…
By other names, strong and stalwart…
By other names, simple and chastened…
And yet, I am one and all the same, neither one of us adversaries, but hallowed nimbi are we…
Your lover forever and eternal for all to see…
Come to me my love, come to me…
Be mine everlasting love's embrace, celestial bliss, set us each other free…

Ω

LAST I SEE

When the autumn day fades away and the leaves fall to grey
When the dying sun shines no more to embered darkened coverlet
When your eyes are no more, the salten tears shorn from that forgotten shore
Such are these nights to be cornered within
Such are these cavernous thoughts without depths
Such are these moments, endless in anticipation
To be within and without...
To watch the rise of the moon in full, the illumined self...
To forget nocturnal rest, oblivion to all...
For these are those moments, those inward stirrings,
Those silences that rustle the grey leaves and let them forever fall.

Ω

CASSIOPEIA

O Queen of Aethiopia…
Wife of Cepheus…
Mother of Andromeda…

O Nereids, behold thy beauty…
Thine own elegance, thine own grace, greater yet…

Decry to Poseidon, O shame…
Must we sacrifice thou ravishing Andromeda…

O Cetus, O Poseidon's beastly serpent, execute Andromeda…

For it is I Perseus riding winged and albicant Pegasus, to your rescue…
Behold Gorgon-Medusa severed head, writhing ophidians…
To stone, horrid, O terrible Cetus, I say…

O friend of Aphrodite…
Is that you my Cassia, née *Kassiopé*, in all your refinery…
For I am Perseus, hero, rescuer, away from Cefeus, for mine own…

On winged horse we fly to azure and cyanic sky…
O Mount Olympus, she is mine…

Is that you my Cassia, for thine is mine…
And mine is thine…
To yonder heavenly cumulus…
Constellation, celestial body, you will not be…
Mine O mine, ever and ever…

O Cassia, you are my queen, to eternity…
Use your sea Nymph magic on me, daughter of Nereus…
Not Andromeda I want, but you my desire, Cassia, my Cassia, my Cassia…
I will not betray thee…

Away we will soar skyward, aloft to the heavenly divine…
My Cassia, sweet Cassia, forever more…

Ω

NIGHT HOPE

As night folds me over in its cape I leave my thoughts for dreams to wake
Only to be alone searching throughout the night
While listening for words unspoken
And weeping for praise never had in glory
Of light unshadowed broken
My eyes gaze upon fragile night
Never to keep stars and moon above
Only in dreaming sleep can I forget the fear
Of what must be, must be
The oncoming of empty light

Ω

ARRANTZALEAK[4]

Remnants of *arrabales*, fishermen's houses whitewashed, crisscrossing wooden gabled-beams, on cobblestone streets, balconies flowered and painted like the *Ikurriña*: red and green, absent Basque flag—some blue…
Gorria eta berdea, urdin batzuk

> Now cafes and bars and restaurants and art galleries…
> Fishermen's boats line the harbour: red and green—some blue and black…

Gorria eta berdea, urdin batzuk eta beltzez

> Some prows, painted coats of arms, some prows with *Lauburu*, four-headed swirling Basque symbol, other symbols still…
> On shore, women selling fish at the fish market, women mending ochre-nets near the port, gossiping—in olden days, women selling sardines in flat-baskets on their heads, *sardineras*—listen to *sardinera* cry out, "fish, fish for sale!"…
> Fishermen's Gipuzkoan ports: Hondarribia, Pasajes, San Sebastián, Orio, Getaria, Zumaia…
> Black-bereted old fishermen gather for rounds of drinks, *txikiteo*…

> Off to sea lads, off to sea! *Itsasoa, Itsasoa, Itsasoa!*

O ancient days, off to Greenland in medieval skiffs, hunting for whales…
O ancient days, off to Greenland and Newfoundland, fishing for cod…

The anchovy catch is low this season…
Gathering seaweed in winter to make ends meet…

Off to fish *atunak*, tunas long-finned and short-finned, silvered torpedoes, frenzied for sardines…
Chum the water! Chum the water lads!…
Spray water from the bilge—frenzied possessed fish, insatiable…
Line up to one side with bambooed rods, hanging silver hooks…
There we go, and up they come, glinting silver in the hot sun…
Gaff them, gaff them, gaff them all…
Deck awash in blood and ocean brine, silver flappings, mouths gaping air…
Let's fill the hull lads! Let's fill the hull!…
Ice them up…
To land, to land, to land we go! *Portura Joan! Portura Joan! Portura Joan!*
Sell them, grill them, *marmitako*…

Ω

PROMETHEUS BOUND

Alas, is it worth giving the world some light?...
Where wrong is wrong, and might is might...
Bounded by Orpheus' song in the dead of night...

Look yonder upon great height...
Forlorn and all alone on precipice...
Try as I may with all my might, I am unable to fight the domain of prejudice...
Awaiting again yet another breaking dawn...
Try as I may, I will not be torn or rent from circumstance facing evermore the
unknown...
Whilst mine own eyes have shown, always the chance, press on, press on...

Alas, is it worth giving the world some light?...
And for most of us shackled and restrained, while for some hanging and caught by
some unending pain...

O great eagle of Zeus, golden in splendour, ever regal but thou bringst death upon
me with your devouring and insatiable bite...

O flight, O flight, away, away...
I need time, please another day...
Do not linger, do not stay, O great raptor, onto Zeus, away I say...
For I am your captor ever more...
Only to Zeus may I implore...
Thus far, he remains deaf, dumb and mute and all the while abstruse...

Alas, is it worth giving the world some light?...
For how much I dare, who will care?...
Now and forever here, alas till one day disappear...

O miserable abyss, ever dark and desolate, never some bliss be had, hopes for
some respite...
Stark and barren rock, tainted with such disdainful hate...
Forever mocked and mere avian bate...

Alas, is it worth giving the world some light?...
All round us yonder is so much fright—a world of suffering, a world of despair, of
miseries—here, there...
Even as day falls into night, it is always best to contemplate on moon's bright glow,
laden opulent blue and white...

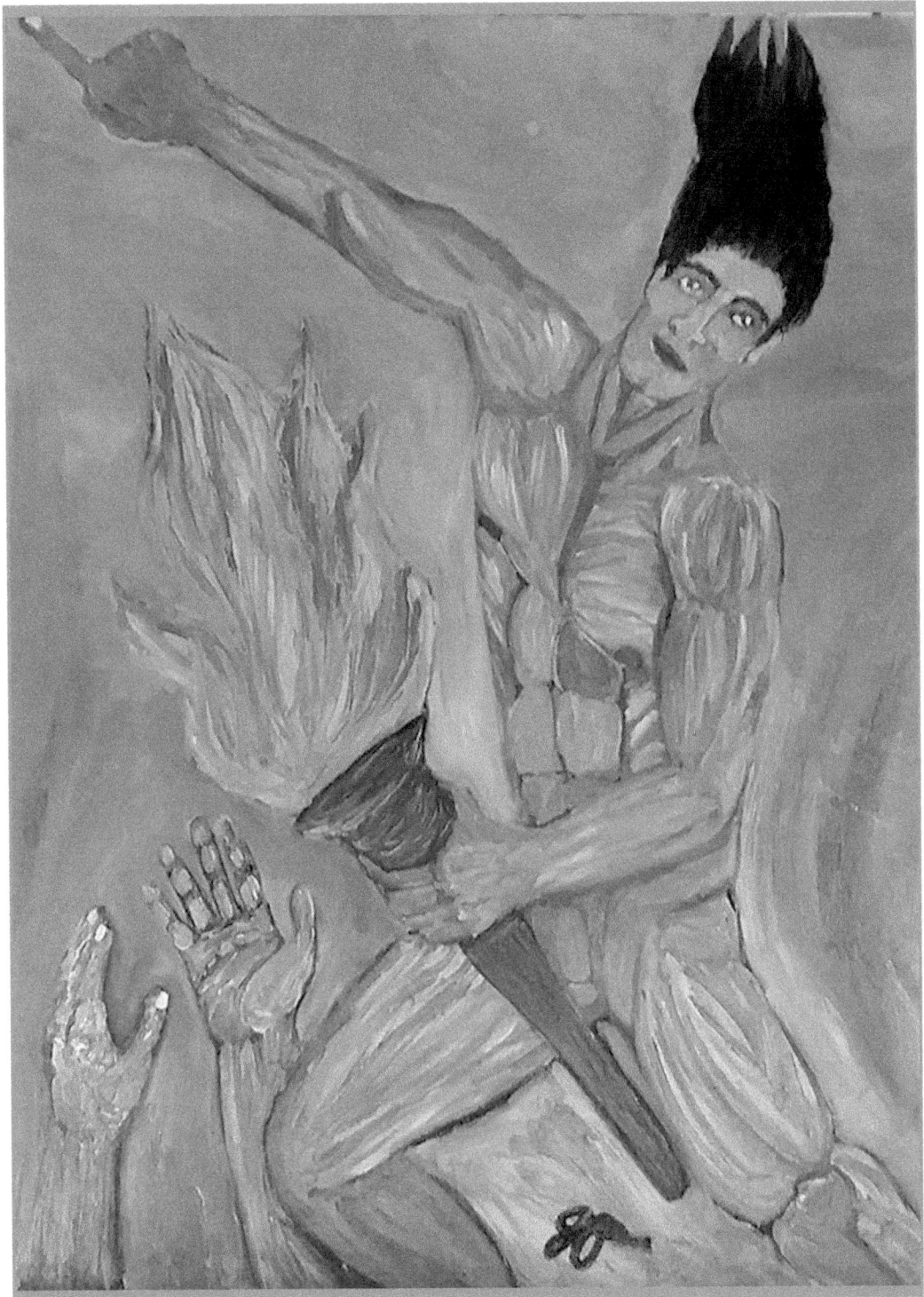

47

Er ne'er to disclaim providence, nor find fault in error…
Some forgotten memories…
And mine own drama, and ne'er denounce thy miseries, thy tragedies nor thy trauma…

'Tis life in the round to never cease in sorrow, though to know there is a morrow…
Chained secure on this here crag, for Shakespeare "all the world's a stage"…
Even so, I am bound, nearly moribund…
Neither strife nor pity, I wish to hear, forbear torture I am compelled…
Even on to the gates of hell…

Struggle onward I must…
Thus, exclaim to the world, illumination proud and true…
Whitened-knuckled, hands clasped behind back, awaiting hitherto another attack…
To be afflicted thus, curled over gaping hole…
E'er more, relive and be regained whole…

An abomination, I think not, mine own reincarnation…
Darkening clouds announce where the great eagle flew…
From Mount Olympus to my abode…
A more horrible sight ne'er to behold…
Not quite, my brilliant luminosity, even if the days run cold, e'er more in sight…

Alas, is it worth giving the world some light?…
To be raised up on this great height, some would have me dashed below…

Till now the world should know, light radiates its glow for minds and hearts alike, to e'er much delight, whence ne'er sate…
An effusion of emotion art doth proclaim, ne'er my plight contrite, mine aim…

To give the world some light, e'er so true, while years and years accrue…

To give the world some light, nay there ne'er has been so much right to eliminate and illuminate all this blight…

$$\Omega$$

O BRASIL

Quiet thoughts through those black eyes, the eyes of the Indians, the gypsies and the Portuguese conquistadors through the ages of the Amazon waters, when the rivers converge black into brown, mud into blackness, time into darkness, they whisper you my love in my dreams, some dreams I have never known but wanted to know for so long…

So are my thoughts of you in the moonlight touching the sand of those white beaches, and laying next to you on that forlorn beach, palm trees swaying beneath that white eye…

Through the red wine, the edge of the water's brine, I see you in the half-blue light, my little one…

Do not run away child of the mountains for I will find you on that forgotten shore, where the jaguar makes his lair beneath the mango trees of that full moon, I will see you move in shadow and feel the silky breeze, your breath upon mine, shadowed paws in patches of half shadow and half light, moving beneath the immense trees darkened in the embankment where the rivers converge and muddied waters run deep and move slowly into blackness and run through your veins little one, I will find you by the moon, I will know where you go…

Child hear the ocean, the waves breaking on the shore, the feel of the moonlight, speak to me with those black eyes and I will be with you forevermore, speak to me with those silent black eyes and Amazon dreams of other worlds and other times when the river runs through you my love, where the muddied water runs into blackness, where your hair sweeps over me in my dreams, speak to me of other times where the jaguar moves in patchy-light, dance with the Indians little one, dance with the jaguar…

Do not run away child of mine for I will find you in the moonlight on that forgotten shore…

Ω

IT IS NEVER ENOUGH

Sometimes time fades away…
>   There are not enough words to say…

Sometimes we are lost and can never be found…
>   Sometimes things are beyond the profound…

There are not enough words to say…
>   Sometimes words are never enough…

To say one is sorry to those we love…
>   In fact, love should be enough…
>   But sometimes words are not enough…

Ω

VALERIA

Memories of you in my dreams…

Where you are I will never know…

You my goddess, you I worship, you alone are my sun…

A house with a white picket fence, lost babies…

Time long gone, the hopes, the dreams…

You my Valeria, you my Boo, you my goddess, you my sun…

You my Hera in you I see my Artemis, your many arrows penetrate me like Saint Sebastian, moon goddess, goddess of renewal and bounteous harvest…

You my Valeria, you my sun…

Where are you now my Boo?

In you I see the world, in you I see the universe eternal…

How the angels and cherubim have blessed you…

To thine flowering laurels on your beautiful crown, flowing black hair, vexing, enchanting eyes…

To thine flowers covering your bodice…

To thine from the foam of oceans and the ever emergent Venus, so far beyond Botticelli, so far beyond the declining Titian, so far beyond the Goyan *maja desnuda*, so far beyond Velázquez' Venus and her mirror…
So divine are thee, to my own, to beyond me, to thine own you will ever be…

In your eyes are the oceans, waves of joy, waves of sorrow, salty tears, Beethoven's 9th symphony…

You are my *Ode to Joy*, you thine with grace, you thou with delicate hands, Michelangelo's Madonna's hands…

In you the eyes of Amerindians, innocent and loving, in you the eyes of gypsies, shifty and cunning, in you the eyes of Portuguese conquerors, piercing and proud…

In you worlds of worlds, in you the star dust of billions of stars, in you the celestial heavens, in you cumulus, in the blue of Magritte, faceless eyes, in you the blue of Matisse, dancing for me like Salome, you breaking into Picasso's cubes, weeping woman, scatter your mind into synaptic firings, into Jackson Pollock's frenzied splashings…

In you supernovas, in you fireworks illuminating the night's sky, cascading shooting stars…

In you the moon, the glowing blue orb, flowing black hair, dark matter of galaxies beyond galaxies, Big Bang ever expanses, infinity, figure 8 horizontal, the Alpha and the Omega…

There you are Valeria and there you are not…

Mine own disintegration in thee, mine own memories, mine own stars, suns, worlds, mine own loss of thee…

Black jaguar, ebony panther, dangerous eyes, ripping claws, pacing in the confines of a cage…

My aurora lights, mirroring stars on dark lakes, equaling energy and mass, so your eyes sparkle speeding past light, *celeritas*…[5]

Orpheus' lyrics, Daphne's distress, Apollo's gaze and everlasting light, you are beautiful after all…

Laughter of children, the laughter in your eyes…

For you know me, for you know I am Elliot's the Hollow Man…

Without you there is nothingness, within you there is being, without you the great void, with you opened curtains to the sun's eternal rise…

In you my conversion, in you the spires and spandrels, in you the great cathedrals of Europe, in you the great Buddhist shrines, in you my Mecca, in you the Holy of Holies…

In you my shaman's mother, in you Gaia, in you chaos, in you Shiva…

In you the root of being, in you the seeds of oaks, sprouting through darkened earth, budding growth, budding love, rising, rising, rising to meet the sun, your sun…

In you the purple shadows of the Grand Canyon, in you the zephyr across the golden wheat, in you the silvery dew of the multitude of spiders' webs spanning countless trees…

The tempest, thy mirror seas, thy heartbeat, thy beating wings of a jade and ruby hummingbird…

Rio Negro, Rio Solimões forked to the Rio Amazonas, bathe me in the Ganges, my ashes thrown from Varanasi…

Red rose petals, thy cheeks, thy sigh, my longing for thee…

Your soft breath on mine, your beauteous sleep…

For I shall sleep no more, nor will I know your paradise, for thine is the kingdom and I am thrown down, a fallen angel, a beast behold, and forever, no more…Gone are you my Valeria…

$$\Omega$$

GRAMPS

Hummingbirds flutter in the dawn,
ruby bellies, fast emerald bodies...
He sits there with his coffee and cigarette enjoying the morning quiet,
contemplating creation...
He knows when the blue jays visit, the orioles, the cardinals and the robins,
all wing their way to his private court...

A sound of the big engine, the flush of the smooth ignition, wheeling around in
comfort of leathered seats in the great car...The 'Pasta King' is here, the hard hat, the
grin, the noise and the constant of maddening humming, the green packages arrayed
and then neatly boxed away, smells of spent wheat...

The buffalo herd of a friend long gone,
the sinewy limbs on the plains near the wild woods...
They gallop now on the plain, churning up the black clots of earth, the bulls snorting
and shaking their shaggy manes...
The loons cry out in the shadows of moonlit waters on the lake...

Here is the dude with his white shirt-sleeves rolled-up and the crack of the baseball
bat, the strong flex of the great forearms...He has a joke, it's a good one you know,
and you'll laugh like hell...the engineer, the orderly mind, the quick temper,
hummingbirds and machinery whirring and whirring to and fro, there and gone, the
rise of the thunderhead, the distant lightening illuminating the shadowy skyline, the
whirring here and there in the twilight of his mind, the eyelids flutter, the laugh still
echoes, the blur of green bodies, those shaking hands of his, the fast-moving
packages off the conveyor belt, a clap of light, a gentle flutter, the whirring hums
gently now, echoes of creation great and small...

Ω

54

INTO THE GREAT RIVER

Along the great river…

Through turbulent white waters…
Jutting black rocks planted dragon's teeth melanic warriors fossilized…
Disjointed atrous bones frozen in time…
Swift rapids Yellow Stone…
Waters running deep…
Over cataracts foaming…
Seething fury-ed leucochroic…
Eruptions tortuous currents pavonated…
Canyon squeezed…
Umbered outcrops…
Jagged white-capped azure mountains…
Coniferous verdant…
Grey men's shoulders…
Like bighorn sheep dead in winter snow jutting rib bones puma eaten…
Like snow covered buffalo buried…
Grey wolf pack howling running madly…
Panicked elk broad candelabra-ed horns…
Virescent Bighorn gentle…
Slate grey snowed albicant mountains castory denuded trees…
Native banshee cries warpainted hundreds…
Violently tumultuous surrounded…
Blued shrieks…
      Winding forking downward
          Diminishing…

     Along the great river…

Rio Solimões Rio Negro confluence…
Black into brown…
Brown into black…
Caboclo cafuzo…
Castaneous Amazon…
Gentle sweeping wide…
Amerindian blood…

Brunneous veins…
Slowly undulating…
Anaconda mother…
Where the Amerindians chant…
Rattle dancing…
Her brown curves…
Animal spirit dreaming ayahuascan…
Feathered warriors jenipapo uruku painted…
Teeming forested river…
Through the virid lushness…
Throaty bird calls…
Macaw screeches Harpy soars…
Profuse greenness…
Smaragdine luxuriant hanging leaves…
Squirrel monkeys chattering howler monkeys bellowing…
Dim sunlit shadows…
Jaguar moving rippling lutescent and ebony….
Spots through the blue shadows…
And she called out to me…
Fleeing brown-footed into corbeau gloom…
Muddied tea-colored…
Dark umbered arms shackled…
Murderous *conquistadores bandeirantes sertanistas*…
O Ciclo da Borracha…
Black Amerindian eyes millennia upon millennia…
Nightmarish miseries oppression conversion disease servitude…
    Sluggish eons…
        Timeless…

    Along the great river…

Ghats to ablutions…
Godly incense….
Marigold garlands prayers…
Acrid sooty aromas blazing crackling…
Ringing bells drumming…
Jacinthe flying embers skyward…
Orange flecks wafting upward…
Inky night…
Ashen bones…

Brahman holies…
Filemot turbid river…
Sludgy murky…
Crocodilian…
White humped bull on bank chewing cud…
Bathing women colorful saris…
To life to birth to life…
Withered white-bearded yogis…
Women gathering caesious water in golden vessels…
Delicately balanced on sari-ed heads…
Ganges of the Hindus…
Meditation devotion…
Buddha contemplation…
Otherworldly Nirvana…

     Into the great river…

Drape me in colored garments…
Gather my marigolds…
Lay me down…
Float away…
Goddess Ganga…
Aarti for you…
Leaved flickering candles…
Lightly lutescent black waters…
Shimmering…
Watery suspension…
     From nothingness…
          Into nothingness…
               And on and on…

Ω

ODE TO RUTH

Fragments of time, blue-light cascading, slight kisses with warm and slender hands
Let the cat purr on your lap once more, let the kittens play with ball and twine
These are my faded photographs, for my memories are such forlorn friends…

How will I see you thence? In the mirror, fixing your hair up,
making yourself elegant for Ed
To dance to Big Band sounds and enjoy your dinner at the club, or somewhere on a
Caribbean cruise…

How will I know you?
Those lonely times at that boarding school with the nuns, all prim and proper…
Or will you be Roaring in the Twenties once more?
Let's do the 'Jitter Bug' to that belting Jazz…

Fix her a Manhattan gents, light her another cigarette will you
See her willowy form move, slim like Katharine Hepburn, tomboyish in slacks
So French, so stylish and yet so German
Sometimes the wry remark, sometimes the stern word,
A love of chocolate, how divine…

How is Pittsburgh in wintertime, industrial arms,
churning out newspaper print in press
Sell the ad, Irish lad, for all to see…

Or to sultry Petersburg and Florida palms, that chocolate-shake I made you order
when you broke your foot
Tell me about family history, our French family in Louisiana, daughter of the
American Revolution…

Prodigal I am, for my strong arms are too helpless to carry your withering self,
yet such feisty and lively spirit
you had, so alive, so alert, such a mind, so quick with words and cross-words,
inquisitions in disquietude
I know you, don't I? Your stories, your love of grandkids, great-grandkids,
baseball scores…

Such golden daughters all three: Minerva, Juno, and Venus left to find Paris' apple
The mythic lullabies and now familied with important careers…golden apples in
your eyes, twinkling selves…

Such love of mysteries, and read them all I see…
Tell me a story when I was young and mischievous…

For how could it be? Oh, grandmamma, how could it be?
Had you heard him sing Danny Boy to you with his angelic choir?
Had you smelled the Irish clover beyond on yonder fields of green?
Had you known that lonely road on that barren hill as it came up to meet you,
so dusty-white amidst the green?
Had you finally said your last *adieu* to the sun as it came to greet you?

What will you whisper to me? Oh, grandmamma, smell of roses, pink and red,
I see the words but I cannot touch them, I see the dream but I do not know it yet in
its watery-shadows
Along that forgotten shore, and onto that green glen,
Let the white-raiment drape you in Camille Claudel's sculpted pose
Let me know you…

For the cat is curled in perfect slumber and I follow that white-dusty road to greet
you, Oh grandmamma…
Wake to those Irish eyes that have come to meet you, wake to those
watery-shadowed dreams in time…

Ω

AND THE DOGS I KNEW

And the dogs I knew…
How I said silly things to you and how you cocked your head that way…
Did you really know what I did say?...

And the dogs I knew…
Mostly English-springers but also a maltipoo or two…
One ran away and ate chicken bones and rat poison, only to die alone and without reason…
Another, just a puppy, ran into a cement mixing-truck, what terrible, terrible luck…
And when they died, I cried and cried…
Enough of sad stories, although very true, I am more interested in their glories, both small and big…
Such as how you played with a ball enthralled, and after my errands, how you did a kind of happy jig, after returning from a short time away…
You were always loyal and never did stray…

And the dogs I knew…
One was a huntress, through and through, lying in wait on a poolside chair, pretending to be asleep, sitting there without a peep…
Then sprang pouncing without announcing on some unsuspecting crow, striking fast with fatal blow—poor, poor, crow…
Most of you liked going after scampering lizards, without hampering your stride, running like a blizzard, my you had so much stalking pride…
Primarily though the dogs I knew loved to go warily after squirrels…
And round and round you whirled at the taunting squirrel, chirping, and hurled yourself at the tree trunk, what must have you thunk?...
Barking and barking to no avail…
Then you went onward marking your trail, whilst also wagging your tail…

And the dogs I knew…
Another of you pressed your teeth against the sliding-glass door in some cartoon smile…
Everyone laughed at you, what a goon all the while…
What you thought, no one could guess, as to what lies behind the canine mind…
It just added to your family lore and what is more you wagged your behind…

And the dogs I knew…
One of you lay at my feet and over my pile of books while doing my Masters…
And all of you had askant looks every time I cooked, to much laughter…
Another of you ran the length of the beach and we had to call you back as you were beyond reach…
All of you were loyal and true, such were the dogs I knew…

And the dogs I knew…
Two of you liked to swim—one in the pool and the other in the ocean…
Your doggy-paddles in fluid motion, swimming to a point and circling back…
Then shaking the water from your back, a whole body shake in encircling water sprays…
While one of you liked to give me doggy-handshakes…
And all of you enjoying the great outdoors, the sun's strong rays, or even if the sun was away that day…

And the dogs I knew…
All of you liked face-kisses with tiny or slobbering tongues, and never amiss when old or young…
One of you liked an untidy crate, your messiness did not abate…
And all of you, never remiss wandering from room to room—zoom, zoom, zoom—in ownership like some warship…
Two doggies I knew did not like the thundering booms-booming some storms did make and shook and shook, and shaked and shaked, with scared and forlorn looks…
One of you liked to play a game, "bally", kick the ball, run, chase it down and return it, dropping at my feet…
What a funny little clown in your own little playground, unconcerned, and always happy to greet…
One of you needed calling after not quite being house-trained, for shame…
Even to our dismay and appalling, we worked on it together all the same, how could we be mad with your caring licks and no glaring faults, nothing to fix…

And the dogs I knew…
All of you loved your treats, any kind met your approval…
At our mealtime our refusal…
One of you sighed while waiting and all of your eyes wanting…
Tried as we may, we could not stop you begging…
But you always laid down by my side…
All of you liked petting…

And all the time I fixed your little bedding…
All of you bounded, around and around, with a favorite toy or bone in your mouth…
All of you suffering from drouth as if you never saw water and panting hotter and
hotter, you little trotter…
Sometimes you annoyed me and destroyed your toys—oh what ploys…
All of you loved the squeaky ones which made squeaky noises…
Playing with your bones in unmistakable growling baritones…

And to all the dogs I ever knew…
I loved each and every one of you…
All of you filled my life with joy…
And if there is an afterlife, dogs will go there too…
All good little girls and good little boys…
Man's best friend, and women's too…
Let's not forget who is who…
All of you loved me unconditionally…
And I loved you more and more additionally…

And to all the dogs I ever knew…
Let there never be a world without you…
To all of you, large and small…
All dogs are love, and love is all…
And if there is any analogue, who cares about an epilogue…
Just between you and me, dogs are people too, just between me and you…

Ω

IN KAFKA'S MIND

In the darkest recesses…
The indignant regresses…
And the constant obsessive, obsessive…

Self-loathing feelings…
Thoughts' growing reelings…
Inquisitions in disquietude…
Attritions in plentitude…

Bureaucrats in shadow plays…
All autocrats' shallow displays…

An insurance technocrat and yet a writer true…
How even then, he knew…

Brooding for the glowing moon…
Alluding to the gloaming and unending doom…

Denials in obfuscation…
Trials without causation…

God, or no?...
Flawed fellow?...

Judaism cloaked from others' racism…
Times of incipient fascism, oceanless atheism, and socialist activism…
Sometimes his animal magnetism and stoic skepticism…

Self-aggrandizing, substitutes (women for fathers), ebony calligraphy…
Womanizing, prostitutes, pornography…
Galvanizing fortitude, permutes with those haunting others, varying enigmatic
iconography…

So many near betrothals, or mere women in brothels…

The Oedipal disapproving patriarch…
The contemptible adducing birthmark…

Burn the notebooks with bonfire, burn them all…
Spurn with an austere outlook mired in earnest thrall, the prodigious godsend,
Max Brod…

Accusations and prosecutions of nonsensical crimes…
Unethical persecutions of nightmarish times…
Epical tragedies without absolutions, perishing in his prime…

Who are the accusers and abusers?…
Conjurers and users of the dark arts?…

Witness black pagan hearts daggered with poisoned arrows…
Tuberculosis sickness, flagrant fictive counterparts, laggard treasons without reason,
dead sparrows…

Tortuous confusions with life's many delusions…
Profusions of doubts and pinioned whereabouts…

The insane and the profane…
Concealed mysteries of the inane…
Lunatic conspiracies which wax and wane…
Heretic histories of great pain…

Obsessions with unknown entities…
Confessions of non-transgressions to nefarious enmities….
Deleterious felonies without apparent remedies…

Shadowed loneliness…
Hallowed obliqueness…
Nonetheless hollowed out to confess…

Transformations into slimy vermin, into bug, into insect…
Damnations through pensively burning, through hallucinations without drugs,
mental malformations hitherto the eternal suspect…

Circumspect frustrations…
Hideous sensations and piteous machinations…

Svelte muscled black leopard…
In hunger knelt, muffled, shuffled, attacked poetic shepherd…

64

Recompense for the offense of starvation…
In defense of deprivation, personal privations…

Ravenous pacing in the cage…
Callous debasing on the stage…

Muted oligarchy of the foreboding fortress…
Disputed citizenry of encoding thoughtless…
Reputed hierarchy of goading conscience…

To the void, to the abyss, to nothingness…
To avoid, to miss, to the senseless…
Devoid, remiss, timeless…
Paranoid, reminisce, oblivion, darkness…
Destroyed, resist unforgiven civilian, hopeless…

Absurd isolation, abject frustration…
Incurred desolation, disconnected narration…

Oppression and repression, living in eternal fear…
Non-intercessions from transgressions, unforgiving, infernal and austere…

Covert depression, horrendous, and ever tragic…
Overt suppression, portentous, and endeavored manic and pathologic…

An elegy to the forlorn and forsaken outcast…
The apogee of him borne to accusations unsurpassed…

Ω

ODE TO MARGARET

Strip the raiment, take down the pig n' cricket from the hearth…
I had watched the shoreline and left the shells where they lay against the grey,
thundering sea that day, happy echoing
voices huddled on their blankets enjoying the sun…
For on that day the forlorn loon cried eerily upon the black-watered lake…

The white-bonnet on the green box, the bonny face, cheeks aglow, black raven hair,
twinkling Irish eyes…

Watch them come around the track, the black clots of earth flying past, the sleek
backs, the bet is on for one among the heaving mass…

Father's mother, daughter of father's mother's father, the inventive wheels churning
out the macaroni spans, the deafening noises of industry moving endlessly forward…

That time of autumn when the geese headed southward so in purposeful black Vs…

Little did I know of those bitter winters she knew so well, the snow in heaps upon
the door, the white blanketing hill to hill, freezing lake to lake…

So much I knew and all the same knew nothing of her, so much in her tender voice
with "dear" after my name, so much in those memories shared, the laughter, the
tears, the growing up with her nearby but far away…

The chiding voice against grandpa's pranks, the multitude of candy bars in the
drawers, the wonderful pies made of wild raspberries and blue berries—all so
wonderful à la mode, quiet gifts, money in cards, surprise checks in the mail…

So much to say of those kisses against warm cheeks, scotch in the glass,
the cold of melting ice against lips…

She rode so well in her younger days, the horse beneath her on green prairie-hills,
the dandelions blowing white in the wind, and that fall on that one day,
shattering dreams of ever riding again…

Then this *Brando* figure rambled along into her life, cigarettes rolled up in
shirt-sleeves, the handsome engineer, followed by six kids, the Catholic family of
one, four boys, two girls, Midwestern dreams…

I knew her most on Easter days at brunches with family about and at family dinners,
and at holiday times, Christmas,
Thanksgivings and on and on, but I knew her most on the phone, so far away yet so
near, some memorable days too, near the beach, bright days, flowers and Easter
bunnies, Easter baskets, the clap of the gentle hand on my hand,
the knowing smile, careful thought out words…

Such motherliness about her matriarchal self, the satisfied smile of grandchildren
running all around and then great-grandchildren too running here and there, the
hugs, the pats on the head, making hotdogs on the lake, cousin gatherings,
mashed potatoes, steaks, trips to a natural history museum near the lake, musty smells,
sister losing her golden shoe off a marina dock,
little brother never still during lengthy brunches, running about…

Upon the ferment against the sea to sift through the scatter of shells left upon lost
shores, the epact of days forgotten in
time, the entrechat of dancing feet, the Irish jig drumming on wooden floor…

Raspberries growing red and black in the undergrowth, the sleek thoroughbreds
nibbling on soft fingers, Murillo's Madonnas, snow drifts near the barren oak,
Irish clover green on the hills of heritage, chants of Latin Mass—avatars all in
waiting transformation…

May we find the lone cricket chirping in the garden, may we find the piglet rooting
in black earth, may we know the call of that white swan on its riverine swim, down
the streams, down the rivers to so many lakes, so many times,
may we know the swifts rising black in the air before an impending storm…

Gentle kiss on the cheek once more, calm the child, gentle pat with gentle hand, pick
the clover gently now, gather up the dandelion,
leave the shells upon that distant shore…

Ω

ODYSSEUS LOST[6]

Onward to Ithaca I go, twelve of my ships in tow…

Onward to Ithaca I go, *kai metá na páo Itháki…*[7]

Tempest coming fast, foreboding, dark, gloomy…

Will I never see my dear Ithaca again, my Penelope, my Telemachus?…

Yearning for wonted life, decade after ceaseless war…

Yearning for sublimity with Penelope and Telemachus, to rule all mine island once more…

Why so Poseidon, impeding, doth obliterating us?

And onward journey in these black seas, rising-ominous-whitecapped, above mast, men afeard, no ramparts for black-ocean, sundered…

For how will I know whence to go, after war, bygone Trojans?…

Alas they knew the wrath of Greeks, trickeries pouring from wooden horse, a successful ploy, breaching gates, valorous men…

And afterwards, King Agamemnon spoke to me triumphant, saying unto me: "cunning Odysseus", *Odysséas ton poniró…*[8]

And yet, I am at wits' end, tempest coming on, men dreading o'er the worst, blinding rains, impairing sight—may we dash upon some isle-crags—with Troy long behind us?…

O good Alexios, my great friend and shipmate, harks to me: "O great Odysseus which way are we to sail for Ithaca yonder? The storm approaches and I am much afeard like the others!"…

"Onward to Ithaca we go," I roar above clap of thunder, "Nor gale nor squall shall impede our way dear Alexios! Hearten our men thus!"…

Hitherto, in Odysseus' mind, harboring fears, thinking alas, "how may I reach Ithacan shores…my beloved Ithaca once more?"…

Will Penelope greet me yonder on that forgotten shore, will Telemachus, now grown, know his father, *patéras* ever more, will subjects bow before me once more?…

Or, shall I be forced upon other shores, other islands, alas forgotten on my Ithacan shore?…

The oracles foretold thine journey, long, treacherous…

What dangers lurk to what future, I know not what…

Poor Alexios, I know not how long we sail, how long will mine sailors bear perils yonder, pondering upon shadowing-heaping blackness…

And impending tempest, blackened clouds O so gloomy-grim, upon our hapless ships, black wolves baying, closing all round, ravenous, possessed, voracious appetites, nothing slaking them…

On they come as Trojan soldiers in fierce lines…wave upon wave, such a war I knew so well…

No escaping this great storm, *megáli kataigida*, these rough-perilous seas, *thalassotarachís*, ships tossing as drunken men with shaky limbs…[9]

Even so, onward to Ithaca I go, "damn Poseidon, damn him!", announced in mine own mind…I must find my Penelope once more…

Her wayward thoughts, absent husband, abandoning her in her solitude on that forgotten shore…

"O Zeus, do not forsake me now, do not forsake us!", Odysseus reasoning, lost in some violently-disturbed reverie, futilely gazing upon herds of a thousand black rams and more, yonder assailing forth…

Onward to Ithaca I go, *kai metá na páo Itháki*, not knowing wherefore…[10]

Will Penelope greet me on that long forgotten shore? Will Telemachus run into mine arms?...

Or, shall I never know that forgotten shore?…

O Ithaca where for art thou, my Ithaca, remember me on that forgotten shore

Ω

MINE OCEAN, MINE OCEAN

Mine Ocean, Mine Ocean…
Indigo, indigo, sapphire, jade…
Tempest swells, black, whitecapped…
Luminescent zig-zagged claps…
Clouds ebonied into grey, Jove's beard…
Puttering flashes, fast drummings, rumblings, far away, gloomy horizon…

Mine Ocean, Mine Ocean…
Debris on a shore, multi-coloured glass shards, opaque-blue-green-orange, seaworn…
Seaweed strewn dunes, plastic six-pack rings, a barnacled flip-flop…

Mine Ocean, Mine Ocean…
Gentle surf rolling to shore...
Whooshing soft shelled-particled sands, white-frothing foam, brine…
Tossed shells in lines, scattered, beige-white-beige, striped, white, pink-tiny
scalloped halves, tiny-red scalloped halves, whelks, halved-conchs-blanched-
exposed-pink-female-genitalia-curves, quartered-moon sand dollar, tiny-halved
mollusks, grey, white, taupe, oatmealed-colours, shells, turkey-wings, lettered-
olives, partial prickly cockles, spotted-slippers, limpets, shark-eyed swirl slippers,
piece of driftwood like an old Indian arm, apple-bitten barnacled-styrofoam buoy
red-white, strands of ochre-coffee coloured seaweed-lines strewn like unwashed
women's hair, tawny-brown, clumps, filaments astray…
Sandpipers, black-white, flitting here, flitting there, quick-quick orange-steps,
following waves to shore, flocking quickly over surf, black-white blurs…
Bubbling sand fleas, buried in thousands, black-tiny airholes line pallid-whitish foam…

Mine Ocean, Mine Ocean…
Glass gleaming calm, mirror seas, glinting steel, burnishing silver…

Mine Ocean, Mine Ocean…
Tidal pools, exposed copper rocks, exposed burnt-umbered algaed-reefs, lunar
recessions, puddled urchins, puddled crabs, puddled hermit crabs, puddled sea
cucumbers, puddled fish in minutiae…

Mine Ocean, Mine Ocean…
Translucent aqua, vast expanses of coral heads, browned-antlers, orange fans,
coloured arrays of reef fish, water-butterflies all, yellow, yellow-blue, red-spider

shrimp, ale-spotted eel gaping hooking-teeth, big-eyed, small-eyed, green parrot fish, red snapper in moving shoals, purplish-spotted cuttlefish dancing, evasion, sudden sepia-discharged cloud, large groupers mouthing in blue shadows…
Orange-white clownfish—cow-like spotted patterns, sifting through swaying anemone tentacles, pink and white, flowerlike stirrings in a breeze…
Barracudas gleaming daggers, ivoried-menacing, silver-blue in long-shadows, blacktipped reef sharks circling, imminent danger, skeletonized galleons on reef's edges, abandoned long ago…

Mine Ocean, Mine Ocean…
Pelagic isles of seaweed, barnacled waste, plastic white-and-blue, bottles, tiny-fish shaded, seahorses jouncing, Gulf Streamed pulling currents northward, blue-swords thrashing at torpedoing tuna, swift great-striped marlins, sleek silvery rapid blue-shadows, flashing sailfish, whipping rapiers, thrashing in currents, breaking surface, quavering-blue shimmerings, splashings…
Mahi-mahi, yellow-gold-green-blue coruscating, after finger mullet, ballyhoos, and pilchards…

Mine Ocean, Mine Ocean…
Sardine runs…
Dolphin bait balls, silvered-metals, gleamings-shinings-blinkings, mail-armoured shoals…
Bull sharks, blacktips, duskies, greys—upward, upward into the fray…
King mackerel, bluefish, swallowing, gulping…
Dive-bombing birds in white-black blurs—diving, diving—downward, downward—cormorants, terns, gulls…

Mine Ocean, Mine Ocean…
Orca pod, black and white breaching, menacing, plumed smoke intermittent…
Hunting, hunting-packs, threatening, terrifying…
Surrounding gray whale calf, push mother away, white plumed spoutings, ocean sneezings, pffffhhh sounding…
Crimson-blue waters…

Mine Ocean, Mine Ocean…
Krill swarms, reddish-yellowy-pink masses, breaching baleen whales, open-mouthing trawlings, black-white penguin projectiles, fur seals, silver fish, frothing surfaces of deep-blue waters…

Mine Ocean, Mine Ocean…
Pinnipeds darting about acrobatic, brown-shadows in bare-lit green-kelp forests…

Gathering fur seals and sea lions on sabled rocks…
Great Whites awaiting, beyond blue shadowed kelp-forests, where abalone lie…

Mine Ocean, Mine Ocean…
Depths upon depths without sunlight, eternal ebonied-night, popping light bulbs,
pulsing glows, green aurora fluorescence-luminescence, translucent lanterns…
Bottom-valleyed, mountains, chasms, smoking sulfur stacks, white crabs, bottom
scavenging worms…

Mine Ocean, Mine Ocean…
A full moonlit night, cyclopean luminous eye, black waters-gentle-white surfaces…
Rise squid rise, mate, milky-puffed discharges, preying snapper, preying grouper,
preying sharks, effervescent frenzies…

Mine Ocean, Mine Ocean…
Oil slicks, plastic refuse islands—barnacled bottles, barnacled cans, barnacled
styrofoam…
Red-beaked puffins, golden tufted puffins, black-white flutterings, bogged down,
suffocating, sticky-black tar, tarred-plumage death…

O pollution, O garbaged seas…

Mine Ocean, Mine Ocean…
Warming seas, dying reefs, dying shoals of fish, dying seabirds…

Where is Mine Ocean?...
How to preserve thee in perpetuity?...
Our Ocean, Our Ocean, it is all for thee, if thee can manage well…
If not—to the dying ghosts in our many seas…
It is not for thee…

Ω

THE ABYSS

You emptied me out into the "Big Empty"…
It was not a sudden emptying either but a gradual one, ever so gradual…
A pouring, a pouring outward…
It was more suspended animation, a trickling stream…
Suspended in space and time…
A hovering of mind over body…
An out of body looking at the body…

You emptied me…
My arms outstretched, legs crossed, emptying into the great ocean…
My arms outstretched, head lolling on the neck, emptying into the nebula…
The purple hazy lighted mist, illuminating my body, hanging over luminous
obscurities…
Above time, above space…
Above myself and within myself…
Above it all…

You emptied me…
Floating and emptying, floating and emptying…
The Dalian Christ above and within a nothingness, an impossible nothingness…
Beyond space, beyond time…
A nothingness of emptying, of emptying out, of emptying within…
Of emptying without…

You emptied me…
Without knowing, you emptied me…
How could you know?
After all, I gave everything to you…
And then you emptied me…

You emptied me…
On my black urn, no self-etchings to be found…
On my black urn, there are no nude figures in auburn silhouette
fighting one another…
Nor are there the gods acting out…

It is a blackened urn, empty…
As black inside as outward…
There is nothing in it to slake my thirst…
There never was…
And there never will be…

Maybe it was I who emptied me after all…
Like "An Occurrence at Owl Creek Bridge" in Biercian fashion, I thought of you…
I thought of an "us", a future us…[11]
Not to be…
I could not look downward…
The downward looking frightened me so…
And yet I struggled there with my feet dangling as such…
Over what?
Space and time suspended me, seemingly forever…
And on and on…

Maybe it was I who emptied me after all…
After all, I had faced the Sartrean "Wall" many times before…[12]
And many times before with the overwhelming feeling of being all alone…
I often touched the emptiness, feeling the sands fall between my fingers,
Languorously…
A fallen multitude of heavens, descending celestial bodies…
Fleeting comets streaking reddish and yellowish, flickering candles…
Snuffing momentary flames of tiny match heads, miniscule, microscopic…
Into oblivion…
Listlessly gazing outward at the blue haze on the horizon…
At the great expanse of the ocean coming onward and onward at me…
Again and Again…

After all it may have been I who emptied me through an act of self-will
Or abnegation…
It is Promethean limbo there, a liminal state…
It is as if I am neither here, nor there, nor anywhere…
But I am here, but I am there too, nonetheless…

After all I have given to the world, the all of it…
And yet wishing to give that much more…
So, in this way, am I suspended by some absent and invisible giant arachnidian design
Beyond me…
Caught in the spandrels of cathedrals spanning the universe…

It is addressing the nothingness in this way…
A kind of telepathy to the eternal eternity…
And in the beyond, beyond, you will find me suspended…
And contemplating in the beyond, beyond…
I am somewhere from the "Big Bang" until now…
And then on and on into the eternal eternity…
Onward so, onward so…
To where I shall never know…

These are only synchronic moments, temporary, dissipating, lapsing, melting…
The will to give them all meaning, the unwillingness to forget…
Are mere words hammered out, sparks flying outward into the oblivion…
Stars being born and stars dying out…
Out of these molten words from Hephaestus' forge…
And yet they are all altogether forgotten…

And there I imagined you…
Hands entwined, bodies entwined…
Writhing ophidian poison, a strangled Laocoön…
Caught up in you, caught up in me, caught up in us, caught up in eternity…

Now, lifting me upward in a manner of the Madonna in mourning…
Arms, outstretched, the Pietà…
A scene, lovely and yet grotesque…
Maybe I allowed you to empty me out…
Maybe not…

I can no longer speak to this void…

Ω

MERE SKETCHES

I took out a piece of fresh waxed paper…
It felt like parchment and I carefully overlaid it…
I began very slowly, ever so slowly, to trace the words…
I wanted to capture each and every phoneme…
I traced each and every morpheme…
I wrote down every syllable, word for word, letter for letter…
Every rhyme…
Every verse…
The diaphanous waxed paper allowed me to map out each letter with pencil…
After I was through, I took my copy of Alfred Lord Tennyson's poem and emplaced
it over my own poem…
It did not fit?…

I tried again and again with ever new waxed paper…
Beginning once more…
Over and over…
This time with Robert Frost, cautiously tracing his letters…
Mindful of each word…
Attempting to capture the cadences of each rhyme…
I erased…
I smudged…
And erased anew…
Then I delicately put the sheet of waxed paper of Frost's poem over my own…
It did not fit?...

I had reams and reams of waxed paper for my tracings and sketches…
I ventured forward…
Striving for more exactitude…
I attentively copied Seamus Heaney, and then Derek Walcott, and then W. H. Auden,
and then the Bronte sisters, and then Octavio Paz, and then Emily Dickinson…
And with each overlay of my poems, they did not fit either?...

With great effort, I worked earnestly on my task…
Again and again with each and every letter…
The pencil carefully marking out each word on waxed translucence…
I overlaid my poems with my waxed sketches of W. B. Yeats, of Maya Angelou, of

Walt Whitman, of Edgar Allan Poe, of Pablo Neruda, and on and on and on it went so…
But nothing fit?…

Paper after fresh waxed paper…
Outlining every verse again and again in utter futility…
But I went onward…
I copied out T. S. Elliot, William Carlos Williams, Elizabeth Barrett Browning,
E. E. Cummings, Langston Hughes, Sylvia Plath, but to no avail…
When emplaced on my poems, there was no match?…

Ever more my pencil shook with greater trembling hand…
Each pencil stroke wanting to gain and absorb the whole of their works…
More and more smudgings…
More and more erasures…
Sometimes the ashen cloudiness of smudgings made the images of words
evermore un-pellucid…
Maddening as it was trying to line up each word and line with mine…

I sketched out the words and verses of Robert Browning, Ralph Waldo Emerson,
William Blake, Lord Byron, Boris Pasternak, Allen Ginsberg, John Donne, Henry
Wadsworth Longfellow…
Each time ever fruitless…
Continually their poems were never congruous with mine…
How could any poet possibly ever fathom to belong to such a pantheon?…
If the words could not be duplicated, what then?…

I broke so many pencils in pure frustration…
Sometimes I punctured the waxed paper and would have to start all over…
I tore up leaf after leaf of waxed paper…
So many times…
But each time, I carefully overlaid the waxed papered traces of their poems over mine…
Each and every line of William Wordsworth, each line of John Keats, each line of
Percy Bysshe Shelley, each line of Alexander Pushkin, each line of Robert Burns, each
line of Charles Baudelaire, each line of Kahil Gibran, each line of Sara Teasdale, each
line of Rudyard Kipling, each line of Samuel Taylor Coleridge, and each line of
Dante Alighieri…

Nothing ever seemed to work in my favor…
With each overlay of waxed paper, the tracings became more and more difficult to read…
More and more pencils were broken on the page in rage…

I sharpened more, their yellowish-black shavings all about the desk…
Pinkish-greyish rubbery-flecks all about the page…
I overlaid poem after poem over mine…
And each time the same result…
The words simply did not match…

It took me such a long time, such a very long time…
Hours and hours I toiled away…
It went on for years and years…
Ream after ream of endless waxed paper…
Smudgings, erasures, smudgings, yet ever more…
Line after line…
Word after word…
Verse after verse…
Rhyme after rhyme…
Attempting to get the lettering just right and so…
Blurry and obscured pieces of waxed papers with my numerous mistakes…
Too numerous to count…

Until one day I just gave up…

Ω

MY LOVE, MY DREAM

my love, my dream…
my love, my dream…

Eros' song, Aphrodite's gaze…

my love, my dream…
my love, my dream…

thunder in your strides amidst the throngs,
bedecked in sparkled jewels, amaze…

my love, my dream…
my love, my dream…

may Orpheus' lyre weep for thee,
to wondrous nature you belong,
like the midday sun do you blaze…

my love, my dream…
my love, my dream…

do you hear the wings of white doves far above
in the cerulean and cream, devoid of flaws with all in awe of
you my love, starlight beaming, so fair without compare…

you my love, you my dream…

Ω

THE RIVER

Be the river…
      I will not change…

Then, be the rock and you will be smoothed over…

Be the river…
      I will not change...

Then be the dead leaf and float along…

Be the river…
      I will not change…

Then be the oak on the bank and watch it pass…
It will pass by you from season to season, from winter to summer…
And on and on…

Be the river…
      But I am me…

No you are one and the same…

How do you know?

        You were once the rock and became smoothed over…

        You were once the dead leaf and just floated along…

        You were once the oak and only a shadow…

But you became the river even though it was years hence…

Flowing onward and onward without end…

Ω

THE FORGOTTEN SHORE

All along that forgotten shore, shall I be with you forever more?

Or, will I fade into memory along that forgotten shore?

Will you ever hold me once more, or shall you discard me, strewn as refuse along that forgotten shore…

Deprived of you, I am hollowed out to my very core, along that forgotten shore…

Your face will I seek to love me once more, or are you walking in shadowed sandprints without owners along that forgotten shore?

Some men would have you and treat you like their whore but these are the faceless and feckless hordes and they did not know you alone and in need of love along that forgotten shore…

How we met as drifters like buoyed glass-bottles bobbing aimlessly amidst the indigo-greenish mashing waves, breaching yonder that bleached and milky sandy-shore with unmarked papers, now loosed from emptied-bottles, and fluttering and scattering to the lost winds along that forgotten shore…

Shall we ever meet again once more, hand-to-hand, feeling wave upon wave, and wet sand wedged between toes, or shall you forsake me and leave me all alone along that forgotten shore?

My mind wanders to times now past, and evening comes, the sun fading fast in crimson and blue-cumuli-ed shadows, and there I stand, old and now neglected and forlorn along that forgotten shore until I shall be no more…

Ω

ENDNOTES

[1] In my poem, "Mayan Memories," it should be noted that the phrase: "They buried us with our eyes wide open" is derived from an interview with a Maya by Paul Farmer (p. 4, 2005) and the quote: "Because the victims had been 'buried with their eyes wide open'." And the rest of horrific genocide stories are from legal depositions I collected and from interviews I conducted. See: Paul Farmer (2005). *Pathologies of Power: Health, Human Rights, and the New War on the Poor*. Berkeley, CA: University of California Press and J. P. Linstroth (2009). "Mayan Cognition, Memory, and Trauma." *History and Anthropology*, Vol. 20, No. 2, pp. 139-182.

[2] Eu canto o seu nome, translation from Portuguese: "I sing your name."

[3] Kypris is the Greek epithet for Aphrodite, goddess of love.

[4] This poem is dedicated to my anthropological fieldwork in the Basque Country of Spain, or Euskal Herria. Arrantzaleak is the Basque word for "fishermen" in the Basque language called euskera. The Ikurriña is the Basque national flag. Mentioned in the poem are the Basque words for different colours (*Gorria eta berdea, urdin batzuk*—refers to the colours, red and green and some blue) and (*Gorria eta berdea, urdin batzuk eta beltzez*—refers to the colours, red and green, some blue and black). The "lauburu", literally means four heads, and is a swirling symbol of four tear drops, symbolizing the four Basque provinces of Araba, Bizkaia, Gipuzkoa, and Nafarroa (some think, originally Celtic in origin). Sardineras are Basque women who sell sardines, at least this was the practice in the past where women walked the streets with baskets of sardines on their heads up until the 1950s. Gipuzkoa is one of three autonomous Basque provinces. The others are Araba and Bizkaia. Tikiteo is Basque for bar hopping. Itsasoa is the Basque word for the "ocean". Atunak is the Basque word for "tuna". Portura Joan in Basque means, "let's go back to the port" or go back to land. Marmitako is a Basque tuna dish, poaching tuna in a tomato sauce with potatoes and other vegetables.

[5] Celeritas in Latin means "haste or speed of action."

[6] Alfred Lord Tennyson wrote the poem about "Ulysses" at the end of his life. By contrast, I wrote a poem about Odysseus or Ulysses at the beginning of his ten year journey to his island of Ithaca from the Trojan Wars.

[7] From the Greek, "Onward to Ithaca I go."

[8] *Odysséas ton poniró*, Odysseus is clever.

[9] Literally from Greek, "great storm" and "rough and perilous seas."

[10] Literally from Greek, "Onward to Ithaca Island I go."

[11] "An Occurrence at Owl Creek Bridge" is a famous short story published by the author, Ambrose Bierce in 1890.

[12] "The Wall" is a short story published by the existentialist philosopher and Nobel Laureate writer, Jean Paul Sartre in 1939.

Ω

AUTHOR BIOGRAPHY

An Adjunct Professor at Barry University, J. P. Linstroth is the author of the book: *Marching Against Gender Practice: Political Imaginings in the Basqueland* (2015, Lexington Books). He obtained a D.Phil. (PhD) in Social and Cultural Anthropology from the University of Oxford with several awards for his research concentrating on the Spanish-Basques. Linstroth was a recipient of two travel grants from the Basque regional government to speak on issues of peace and conflict resolution in the Basque Country (2005 & 2006) and a signatory of the Brussels Declaration for Peace to end ETA violence (2010).

He was a co-recipient of an Alexander von Humboldt Foundation Grant (2005-2007) to study immigrant populations in South Florida, Cubans, Haitians, with particular emphasis on Guatemalan-Mayan immigrants. Furthermore, he was awarded a J. William Fulbright Foreign Scholar Grant (2008-2009) to study urban Amerindians in Manaus, Brazil and to be a Visiting Professor with the Department of Anthropology at the Universidade Federal do Amazonas (UFAM). His main academic research interests are: cognition, ethnonationalism, gender, genocide, history, immigrant advocacy, indigeneity, indigenous politics, indigenous rights, memory, peace, peacebuilding, racism, and trauma. Linstroth is also an artist. His paintings have been shown at various venues in Palm Beach and Martin Counties, Florida. *The Forgotten Shore* (2017, Poetic Matrix Press) is Linstroth's first book of poetry.

Ω

www.ingramcontent.com/pod-product-compliance
Lightning Source LLC
Chambersburg PA
CBHW080546090426
42734CB00016B/3217

9780998146973